A Platonic Theory of Epistemic Value

By

Joseph Andrew Barnes

Abstract

Why is knowledge better than mere true belief? To make progress in answering that question, we need to distinguish two ways to understand it. It might mean: why is knowledge *epistemically* better than mere true belief? Or it might mean: why do we have reason to prefer epistemically better beliefs to epistemically worse beliefs? In the same way, the question "why is a Ferrari better than a lemon?" might mean "why are good cars better *as cars* than worse cars?" It might be, that is, a request for a general theory of car-wise goodness. Or it might instead be asking why car-wise goodness matters: "why prefer a good car to a bad one?"

Why is knowledge epistemically better than true belief? According to plausible accounts, the epistemic value of a belief is a matter either of the likelihood that it is true or its degree of support by one's total evidence. These accounts, however, can't make sense of some comparative epistemic evaluations. They must treat the Churchlands' philosophically reasoned belief that there are no beliefs as epistemically just as bad as a wikipedia reader's rash belief in the same proposition, although intuitively it is epistemically better. And the plausible accounts must treat some beliefs in "commissive" versions of Moore's paradox, such as "it's raining, but I believe it's not raining," as epistemically ideal, though intuitively they are not.

What these plausible accounts overlook is that the epistemic value of a belief is in part a matter of *how influential* the evidence for it is: how it might affect what the total evidence of *other* believers supports. This "discursive epistemic value" is what the Churchlands' beliefs have, and what all commissive Moorean beliefs lack. The Churchlands' evidence is more influential than the freshman's, whereas the commissive Moorean believer's evidence can never be maximally influential.

Discursive epistemic value also helps answer the second question, by solving "the Meno Problem." Roughly, the Meno problem is to explain why we have reason to prefer knowledge to mere true belief, given that they are in some sense practically equivalent. The standard explanation is that knowers are more likely to retain their true beliefs in the future. But this explanation is unsatisfying, since it seems to make the epistemic status of the knowledge otiose. After all, if knowledge were preferable only as a means to further true beliefs, then the epistemic status of knowledge would be dispensable. In contrast, on my account, it is precisely the epistemic status of knowledge – and in particular its discursive epistemic value – which makes knowers more persuasive and qualifies them to teach.

Of course, knowers are not always more persuasive. So discursive epistemic value does not always give us reason to prefer knowledge to mere true belief. But that is, I argue, as it should be. We do not always have reason to prefer knowledge to true belief. Epistemic goodness *amplifies* reasons for or against having a true belief. So, in general, only when we have reason to prefer having a true belief to lacking it do we have reason to prefer an epistemically good true belief to a mere true belief. By contrast, when we don't have reason to prefer a true belief in the first place, we often actually have reason to prefer that it be epistemically *bad*. For instance, the depressive's self-destructive belief about his own mediocrity is all the *worse* for being supported by influential evidence.

In addition to other applications, discursive epistemic value affords an satisfying internalist response to an externalist demand. How, externalists may demand, are internalist requirements conducive to anything of epistemic value? If I am right, the internalist may reply: they are conducive to discursive epistemic value.

Table of Contents

Introduction – What Good Is Knowledge?
p. ii

Chapter 1 – Value and Epistemic Value
p. 1

Chapter 2 – Meno Problems
p. 22

Chapter 3 – The Swamping Problem
p. 39

Chapter 4 – Two New Problems
p. 54

Chapter 5 – Discursive Epistemic Value
p. 72

References
p. 87

Appendix I – Skepticism about epistemic value
p. 90

Introduction.

Why is knowledge good? The kind of answer I've most frequently heard from non-philosophers cites particular examples of enormously useful knowledge. For instance, knowledge of the enigma code gave the allies a great advantage in the second world war.

It is certainly true that being motivated by accurate information about the enigma code was advantageous. But that is unlikely to answer the question that philosophers have in mind. After all, their question is about knowledge in general. Sure, some bits of knowledge – secrets, let's call them – are very important, and coming to have them will better your position. But that's also true of lottery tickets. If you've got just the right one, it will better your finances. The problem is that both winning lottery tickets and secrets are few and far between. "Buy a lottery ticket" would be bad advice for someone struggling to improve their finances. Why should "strive for knowledge" be any better advice?

Another fault philosophers will find with this answer is that knowledge is not the only thing that can make us act. The enigma cryptographers could have acted on mere beliefs, or educated guesses. As long as they were aware of the secrets, and had full confidence that they were right, they would have done roughly the same as they did do. Perhaps knowledge would have made some difference. But the point is that knowledge is not necessary to make the big strategic difference that makes this seem to be such a good example of the power of knowledge. True belief would suffice for many purposes, including many of the cryptographers' purposes. So not only do striking examples like the enigma code not give us an answer about why knowledge in general is good, they don't seem to give us examples where it's clearly *knowledge* that is good. The cryptographers might have merely believed what they knew. It is *what* they knew that put them in an especially good position, rather than that they *knew* it.

So we might want to reformulate the question in two ways. In order to capture the specificity of our initial question about knowledge, we might ask "why is knowledge better than true belief?" And in order to control for the atypical value of knowing secrets, we might reformulate the question with an explicit quantifier: "why is each instance of knowledge good?" If we put these questions together, and specify that we're interested in propositional knowledge, we get the question: "why is knowing that p better than merely truly believing that p, for each p?"

This is the question that has attracted most attention, and it is the question I take up in the dissertation. But it is important to see, I think, that one plausible and interesting answer to the starting question has been simply ruled out by this reformulation of the question, which is very common in the philosophical literature.

Suppose that, for some particular p, knowing p turned out to be no better than merely truly believing p. That would show that there can be no general answer to the reformulated question – that it is a request for explanation of something that is not true. But would it show that there is no good answer to the original question – would it show that knowledge is not good? I think not. It might be that we highly and correctly value coming to be aware of secrets. And it might be that we are more likely to come to be aware of secrets by aiming at *knowledge*. Not merely aiming at knowledge of the secret, but aiming at knowledge in general. In this case, we might say that knowledge is good because aiming at it makes you more likely to come to be aware of secrets. Of course, for any particular secret p, it need not be the case that knowing p is any better than merely truly believing p. The point would just be that, if you want to come to be aware of, say, the secrets of the universe, you're better off doing science rather than astrology. If you want to crack the enigma code, you're better off doing math rather than LSD. That's not because you come to *know* what you find out, but because you're more likely to find out something useful if you go about your inquiry in ways that frequently result in knowledge. Knowledge is a valuable as the necessary byproduct of an activity that is instrumentally valuable for coming to be aware of secrets.

As far as a practical justification for funding careful scientific research, this seems to me more important than anything I'll say in the dissertation. And it is just one plausible justification of many other possible *content-focused* explanations of the value of knowledge, where the explanation connects our interest in learning privileged content, like secrets, to the epistemic practices of so-called knowledge producers.

But epistemologists aren't just worried about justifying careful scientific research. They're concerned to make the case that knowledge is good not solely as a by-product of the best process of finding things out, but also in itself. And in order to satisfactorily address that concern, we need an answer to the reformulated question: why is knowledge that p better than mere true belief that p?

It's natural to think that the answer to this question has something to do with a special connection to the truth. I'll call these accounts *truth monist* accounts of epistemic value, following established usage. But the central contention of this dissertation is that truth monist accounts of the value of knowledge leave something out. In particular, they leave out something about the role knowledge plays in human societies, where it distinguishes the savant from the ingenue, the teacher from the student, and the philosopher from the sophist.

There are, of course, many different ways to develop the story of how our concern for truth relates to our concern for knowledge, since there are many ways to develop the story of how knowledge relates to truth. The most plausible of these, it seems to me, is to introduce evidence as an intermediary, so that in the broadest and roughest of outlines, the story is that knowledge requires having evidence, and having evidence makes truth more likely in two ways. Having evidence for our present beliefs makes them more likely to be true. And having evidence for our present true beliefs makes us more likely to retain those true beliefs into the future.

This is probably part of the story about why knowledge matters. But a lack of clarity about what it means to say that knowledge matters can make it look like the whole story. So in Chapter 1, I clarify the question "why is knowledge that p better than mere true belief that p?" Some talk about the value of knowledge is about the specifically epistemic value of knowledge, which matters to what we have reason to *believe*. Other talk about the value of knowledge is not about reasons for belief, but is about reasons to *desire* knowledge. This is not a question about specifically epistemic value, but about value in general.

There are hard questions about why we even have reason to desire true beliefs, let alone knowledge. But Chapter 2 I take up a question more central to epistemology: supposing that we do in general have reason to desire true beliefs, why do we have reason to prefer knowledge to mere true beliefs? This problem is known in the contemporary literature as the Meno problem. But here, too, the apparent unity of the problem breaks down on reflection. There are many Meno problems. And the special connection that knowledge has to truth – in this case, to future true belief – does not solve the more interesting problems. What does solve the more interesting problems are some of the practical benefits of knowledge which are more specific to its epistemic standing – in particular, the social abilities that come with having good evidence for beliefs, such as abilities to teach and persuade.

In Chapter 3, I consider a challenge to the truth-centric account of specially epistemic value, known as the Swamping Problem. The idea is that, if epistemic value is a matter of a special connection to the truth, then nothing can be *more* epistemically valuable than the truth. So knowledge could be no epistemically better than true belief. I argue that, properly understood, the swamping problem does not refute truth-monist accounts of epistemic value, though it does constrain how the view is formulated.

However, in Chapter 4, I present two counterexamples to truth-monist accounts of epistemic value. In both counterexamples, two individuals are precisely parallel with respect to how well their evidence supports their beliefs, or how likely their beliefs are to be true, but there is intuitively a difference in the epistemic value of their beliefs. An intuitive case of this kind pits a reflective clairvoyant (who knows that he is reliable) against someone with a well-worked out predictive theory. Suppose they both believe p, and their beliefs are equally likely to be true. Isn't the belief which is supported by a well-worked out theory epistemically better?

The obvious objection is that this difference is also a difference in how well their evidence supports their belief. In order to surmount this objection, I present two cases where I am free to stipulate how well the believer's evidence supports their beliefs. For instance, where there is no bar to how well the believer's evidence support her belief, I am free to stipulate that a believer's evidence supports her belief in the proposition in question as well as possible. Nonetheless, in some cases of Moore's paradoxical beliefs, such as "I believe it's raining, although it's not," the beliefs seem to be epistemically worse than other beliefs which are equally well supported. Liminal cases like this are more compelling counterexamples, even if they are not as immediately intuitive.

If the difference in epistemic value between these beliefs isn't due to a difference in their support by the believer's evidence, what does make the difference? In the final chapter of the dissertation, I offer an account of discursive epistemic value, which is a matter not of how well a believer's evidence supports their beliefs, but a matter of how influential their evidence is. The problem with both the Moorean believer and the clairvoyant is that their evidence is insufficiently influential. Evidence is more influential when it is open to inspection in ways that a well-worked out theory is, and clairvoyance is not. Thus the clairvoyant's belief may be equally well supported by her evidence, but the same belief, held by others, would not be as well supported by the clairvoyant's evidence as it would be by the evidence of the well worked-out predictive theory.

Having influential evidence is one factor that enables people to teach. Thus discursive abilities, like teaching and persuading, turn out to be an important part of the answer to both the questions distinguished in Chapter 1. Part of our reason to desire things of epistemic value, like knowledge, is that some epistemic value is discursive, and having cognitive states with exceptional discursive epistemic value enables one to teach. Knowledge is worth wanting, in part, for social reasons.

There are several reasons why this account of epistemic value matters, but two of these reasons bear remarking on here in the introduction, although I don't develop these thoughts in the dissertation.

First, this is a Platonic theory of epistemic value. It recognizes the special epistemic and practical value of the episteme that Plato's philosopher-king has, and takes its inspiration from Plato's remarks on teaching in the *Meno* and elsewhere, as well as the account of the philosopher-king's knowledge in *Republic* VII. And it offers a charitable explanation of some of Plato's criticisms of perception, since perception is in the relevant way like clairvoyance. In other work I do the interpretive work required to argue that something close to the theory I defend is genuinely Platonic. This dissertation is sadly not the place for that interpretive work.

Second, discursive epistemic value also offers a compelling internalist response to an externalist objection. One way for an externalist to respond to an internalist requirement on justification or knowledge is to ask how that requirement is conducive to anything of epistemic value. For instance, Alston asks how Foley rationality is conducive to truth; since he concludes that it is not truth-conducive, he concludes that Foley rationality is not a requirement on epistemic justification.[1] But if truth, or likelihood of truth, or support by total evidence, is not the only thing of epistemic value, then the internalist can respond to this externalist objection by pointing to discursive epistemic value as what their internalist requirement promotes.

It's important for an internalist to have some response to a line like Alston's, because many people have agreed with Alston that truth is in some special way central to epistemology. And if you agree with Alston about that, then it can be hard to see why the sorts of things internalists get excited about have anything to do with epistemology. Of course, I hope my account of discursive epistemic value is correct. But even if it turns out to be flawed in its particulars, I hope it will serve to illustrate a much-needed corrective for this externalist mistake.

---

1   See Chapter 1, esp. footnote 10.

Chapter 1: Value and Epistemic Value

Why is knowledge better than true belief? Although that question is at the heart of the burgeoning literature on epistemic value, it seems to me to be poorly understood. In this chapter I try to clarify what the question means.

In order to understand talk about epistemic value, it's important to first get clear on what is meant by "value" here, and then to get clear on what "epistemic" contributes to the phrase "epistemic value." Once we're clearer on what epistemic value is, it will become clear that we conflate two distinct questions, when we ask why knowledge is better than mere true belief. One question is about a special kind of value – epistemic value. Does knowledge have more of this special kind of value than mere true belief? The other question is, roughly, whether knowledge is worth wanting. This is not a question about a special kind of value. It asks, instead, how knowledge integrates with other things of value.

Although these are distinct questions, the answers to them would go together, if everything of epistemic value were also worth wanting. But I will argue that not everything of epistemic value is worth wanting. Thus an adequate theory of epistemic value need not be compatible with the proposition that all knowledge is worth wanting,[1] and the two questions must be pursued separately. In Chapter 2, I take up the question why knowledge is worth preferring to mere true belief. In Chapters 3 through 5, I take up the question of why knowledge is epistemically better than true belief.

I.   Evaluations & value.

Evaluations are sentences which seem to say that something has some value, or is in some way good or bad.[2] The simplest way to say so is by predicating those very words of something: "Knowledge has value" or "Saving grandmothers is good" or "That move was bad." But the simplest way is not the only way. "Killing is never justified" and "Unfortunately he's eating it" also seem to say that killing in general or a particular episode of eating is bad, whereas "Socrates benefits the Athenians" seems to say that Socrates is (or some of his actions are) in some way good.

Claims about justification or rationality are generally thought to be like these less simple claims, in that they say that something is in some way good. So, for instance, "Bea's bet was irrational" or "Abe unjustifiedly insulted the chief" both are generally counted as evaluations. Since "evaluation" in this sense is a technical term, and the most paradigmatic epistemic evaluations are about justification and rationality, I'll follow this usage of "evaluation."

On one standard usage of "value," values are truthmakers for evaluations.[3] So, if there are

---

[1] Kvanvig 2003, inter alia multa, suggests that an account of the value of knowledge constrains an account of the nature of knowledge (e.g. "An account of the nature of knowledge incompatible with its value would be problematic", on p. x).

[2] Making this notion precise seems to be as difficult as making precise the more general notion of what a sentence is about; in what follows nothing depends on the classification of what might be thought to be borderline cases of evaluations, e.g. "this thermostat is working." I do rely, though, on the idea that non-evaluations can embed evaluations, as for instance in "Bea thinks that pie is good."

[3] "Truthmaker" here is not intended to be theoretically loaded; the point isn't intended to bear more weight than an analogy might, to the effect that values are to evaluations as birds are to claims about birds. For different sorts of claims, the relationship of birds to claims about birds may be different, but the intuition that there is *some* important relationship in each case is strong, even if giving an an account of the systematic relations between truths and

some true evaluations, and if there are some truthmakers for them, then there are values. If there aren't, for instance because evaluations are not truth-apt, then there are no values. Of course, even if there are values in this sense, there will be further semantic questions about the precise content of the evaluations, such as whether their content is representational. And there will be metaphysical questions about those values: what sort of things those truthmakers are, whether they do or don't fit with certain pictures of reality, and so on. But, on this usage, if indeed there are some true epistemic evaluations, then there are epistemic values.[4]

Although this is in some respects a strange use of "value," it seems to me the most enlightening place to start, at least with regard to debates about epistemic value, because all parties can agree that there are epistemic values, in this sense of epistemic value. For this reason, when I talk about epistemic values, this is what I will mean: truthmakers for epistemic evaluations.[5]

II. Epistemic Value

In order to understand claims about epistemic value, we have to understand which evaluations are epistemic. A rough handle on this is easy to come by, using the contrast between epistemic and pragmatic reasons for belief. Whatever the pragmatic benefit of belief in god, Pascal's wager wouldn't give you *epistemic* reason to believe in god, and so wouldn't make you *epistemically* justified in believing in god, even if it would give you pragmatic reason, or make that belief pragmatically justified. So epistemic evaluations aren't just: evaluations of beliefs. They include only a subset of all evaluations of beliefs, and exclude some pragmatic evaluations of beliefs.[6]

That rough and easy handle is also imprecise and negative. Unfortunately, a precise positive account of which evaluations are epistemic is not easy to give. Nonetheless, some positive things are relatively clear. Even the contrast between pragmatic and epistemic justification seems to assume that evaluations of a belief as epistemically justified are epistemic evaluations. So paradigmatic epistemic evaluations evaluate a belief as epistemically[7] justified or unjustified. To say that a belief is

---

truthmakers is hardly trivial, and even if there turn out to be insoluble problems for some accounts of the relations involved.

4   In the appendix, I offer a criticism of any view that denies the existence of epistemic values in this sense, similar to but more plausible than the similar version given by Kvanvig 2003, pp. 174-6. The criticism is that any such theory is non-self-recommending. Whether or not this is a genuine criticism depends in part on what is of epistemic value – in particular, on whether a truth-monist view of epistemic value, which I articulate in Chapter 3 and attack in Chapter 4, is adequate. Note that Carter and Chrisman 2012 defend "epistemic expressivism" from Kvanvig's argument by abandoning the traditional expressivist claim that evaluations are not truth-apt. I do not take the argument in the appendix to afflict contemporary expressivist views on which the evaluations would be truth-apt, e.g. Gibbard 1990.

5   My aim here is to clarify one particular debate, and my excuse for this terminological fiat is that these usages do, I think, clarify it. In particular, there's a tension between two ways in which epistemology is supposed to be normative: (1) in its vocabulary, which is the sense that this sense of "value" captures and (2) in some more substantive way. But in the literature the distinction between (2) and (1) is often swept under the carpet. And this usage makes more explicit the difference between claims that follow from normative vocabulary ("merely evaluative" claims) and more substantive normative claims. Of course, clarifying one set of issues may obscure another, and I wouldn't claim that this is the best way to capture, for instance, disputes between consequentialists and deontologists, let alone to have settled any other disputes by terminological fiat. For all I've said here, Scanlon's buck-passing account could be a better account of values in general.

6   I am tempted to say that they exclude *all* pragmatic factors, but that is a subject of dispute. Proponents of "pragmatic encroachment," discussed below, take *some* pragmatic factors to be relevant to epistemic evaluations. But no-one, I take it, would claim that Pascal's wager gives us *epistemic* reason to believe that a divine rewarder exists.

7   Henceforth I'll drop this cumbersome qualification, but it should be understood in all references to justification

justified is to evaluate it positively; to say that it is unjustified is to evaluate it negatively. But, by almost any account, these are not the only kinds of epistemic evaluation, since one may also evaluate a cognitive state positively by calling it knowledge, or by saying that someone knows something, or by saying that it is epistemically rational or supported by evidence. Even theorists who wouldn't include these notions in their analysis of justification would presumably admit that they are nonetheless epistemic.

In addition to these paradigm evaluations, there is a kind of penumbra of evaluations which are plausibly, recently, and widely, though not universally, thought to be epistemic. Even if a particular philosophical account of justification is mistaken, one might think the failed analyzantia nonetheless capture *some* kind of epistemic evaluation. For instance, one might think that Foley rationality[8] is a poor analysis of justification, but nonetheless think that to say that someone's belief is Foley rational is to evaluate it positively, and in a specifically epistemic way.

There are also some outlying evaluations, which might be plausibly thought to be epistemic, although they are less widely and recently thought to be the concern of epistemology proper, as for instance Kvanvig's "objectual understanding,"[9] e.g. "she understands quantum mechanics" or evaluations involving Platonic and Aristotelian ἐπιστήμη or νοῦς, e.g. "the philosopher-king has ἐπιστήμη."

Finally, there are some claims in the literature which are clearly epistemic, and clearly evaluations: claims about what one *epistemically ought* to believe. But because it's not at all clear what these claims mean, they won't help us with the question at hand. That is, they won't help us understand which *other* evaluations are epistemic. In section IV I'll return to epistemic ought claims and consider what they might mean.

Problems for paradigm cases

In the rest of the dissertation, the arguments depend only on the epistemic-ness of the paradigmatic epistemic evaluations: claims about whether and to what extent a belief is justified, or rational, or evidentially supported. But one might worry that even some of these paradigmatic epistemic evaluations are not, strictly speaking, epistemic.

One sort of worry simply takes a view of epistemic value and attempts to build it in to the criterion of epistemic-ness. Alston, for instance, argues that Foley rationality and any other putative analyzantia of justification fail to be properly *epistemic* notions if they fail to be truth-conducive.[10] But truth-conducivity is a poor guide to our practice of epistemic evaluation, as I'll argue in Chapter 4. Some beliefs are truth-conducive but are intuitively epistemically bad, for instance. So not only would Alston's move be question-begging in this context,[11] it would also present a distorted picture of the evaluative practice Alston aims to capture.

---

unless otherwise specified.
8   A belief is Foley rational for S roughly iff S would believe it after engaging in Cartesian Meditation. Full account in Foley 1987, esp. p. 66.
9   e.g. in Kvanvig 2003.
10 Alston 2005, esp. pp. 45-47. In short: "It is reasonable to take these [non-truth-conducive things] as being goals of cognition that are partly independent of any connection with the goal of truth...But since their intrinsic value as aims of cognition is independent of the aim of true belief, why should we count these items as *epistemic* desiderata on the criteria I have been using for that? If we have a reason for doing so, it is that they also have an essential relation to true belief..." (p. 46).
11 Alston 2005 presents this consideration only after arguing that "justification" is not adequate to the task of discriminating the epistemic evaluations from non-epistemic evaluations, so that truth conducivity wins, since it is the only plausible alternative. In Chapter 3, section I, I argue that justification is adequate to that task.

Another sort of worry separates out some subset of the paradigm epistemic evaluations as capturing what is really epistemic. For instance, one might argue that rationality does not coincide with justification, and is properly speaking epistemic only when it does coincide with justification. However, though this might give us a not implausible account of what certain epistemologists have investigated, surely that reflects the boundaries of their investigations, and not the boundaries of the properly epistemic. In any event, nothing here or in what follows will depend on intuitions about rational but unjustified beliefs.

Another similar but much more serious worry motivates narrowing the range of epistemic evaluations in order to avoid pragmatic encroachment. Suppose that ordinary ascriptions of justified belief and knowledge are sensitive to pragmatic factors,[12] and these ordinary evaluations are not systematically mistaken. But, one might think, properly epistemic evaluations are not sensitive to pragmatic factors! After all, pragmatic benefits attached to believing p don't in general make that belief rational – that's the "rough handle" intuition with which we started. So, one might infer, pragmatic benefits can't *ever* be a difference-maker to the properly epistemic status of a belief. After these reflections, one might conclude that it is not justification properly speaking which is epistemic, but that justification is a hybrid notion, sensitive both to properly epistemic factors like the quality of one's evidence and to non-epistemic factors like how important it is to get the belief right. The non-epistemic factor determines how good your evidence needs to be, in order to count as justified in a particular context. But the only properly epistemic factor is, according to this line of thought, only the quality of your evidence. In a discussion of the semantics of "knows," Richard Feldman voices a parallel suggestion:

> "[The debate about skepticism] is a debate about how good our evidence is. Understood that way, it is difficult to see the epistemological significance of decisions about which standards are associated with the word 'knows' in any particular context."[13]

Feldman's idea is that, if "knows" is sensitive to pragmatic factors, then it is not a purely epistemic concept. Instead, it is a hybrid notion in the same way that justification might be thought to be, if "epistemically justified" turns out to be sensitive to pragmatic factors. Now, if "knows" attributes knowledge, and knowledge is not strictly speaking epistemic, one might justly wonder what state could possibly be better qualified as an epistemic state. Fortunately, since none of the arguments to follow turn on any pragmatic factors making a difference to epistemic evaluations, this is another debate into which I need not enter here.

However, the worry about pragmatic encroachment seems to generalize. Suppose that ordinary ascriptions of justification turned out to be sensitive to moral factors. Surely in that case they would have to be factored out of the account in order to get to the properly epistemic core of justification. After all, moral factors have no more to do with the quality of evidence than pragmatic factors. But, then, is there anything that has to do with the quality of evidence other than, well, the quality of our evidence? So, if this reflection is compelling, it's hard to see how we can stop short of shrinking the domain of epistemology down to the study of evidence.

This narrow conception of epistemology is potentially a problem for the counterexamples I offer in Chapter 4. For those counterexamples will involve cases where there is no difference in how well someone's evidence supports their beliefs, but there seems to be a difference in the epistemic standing of their beliefs. But if the narrow conception is right, that apparent difference in

---

12 Argued by Fantl & McGrath 2002, Hawthorne 2004, & Stanley 2005.
13 Feldman 2004, p. 32.

epistemic standing must be an illusion: either there is a difference in evidential support, or the difference simply isn't epistemic.

To insist on the narrow conceptions of epistemology and the quality of evidence, in the context of the argument in Chapter 4, would be question begging. While the counterexamples in Chapter 4 are cases where two believers' beliefs are equally well supported by their own evidence, there are still differences in the quality of their evidence. It is these differences in the quality of their evidence which, on the account in Chapter 5, matter to the epistemic standing of their beliefs. So, provided that we have a liberal conception of measures of the quality of evidence, the narrow conception of epistemology does not threaten anything I'll say in Chapters 4 and 5. Nonetheless, question begging or not, the narrow conception of epistemology is so well entrenched that a bit of softening up is in order.

Broadening considerations

Nonetheless, it's worth thinking seriously about the narrow conception here, since it coheres with a common view of epistemic value, and might threaten a liberal conception of the measures of the quality of evidence. And there are some good reasons to resist the narrow conception.

On the narrow conception, all properly epistemic evaluations attribute one of a very limited number of statuses (justified, unjustified, rational, irrational,[14] evidentially supported, evidentially unsupported, knowledge, not knowledge) to one kind of object: beliefs.[15] So there are at least two ways in which the class of epistemic evaluations might be broader. It might include evaluations of things other than beliefs; and it might include the attribution of other statuses, whether to beliefs or other things. If "that belief is Foley rational" counts as epistemic, that would expand the narrow view to include a new epistemic status, namely Foley rationality. If "her theory is evidentially supported" counts as epistemic, that would expand the narrow view to include a new object of epistemic evaluation, namely theories.[16]

It's worth noting that the narrow conception is not as widespread as it might seem. For instance, many philosophers take themselves to be making epistemic evaluations of degrees of belief, although they think that these are not definable in terms of belief.[17] Such philosophers clearly do not think that beliefs are the only object of epistemic evaluation.[18]

The most trenchant problem with the view, it seems to me, is that although the contents of beliefs are propositions, we seem to make the same sorts of evaluations of states whether or not

---

14 Subject, of course, to earlier worries about "rational."
15 "Beliefs" here is used generically to cover suspension of belief and disbelief.
16 It won't always be clear how the inclusion of a given sort of evaluation would broaden the class. For instance, some people think that knowledge states are not simply a subclass of belief states; if they aren't, then the narrow view as spelled out here has a close cousin according to which there are two fewer statuses and two more objects. The same sort of problems will afflict evaluative verbs like "to understand," "to recognize," and so on. For my purposes here, there's no need to settle these issues.
17 I take it this is not contentious: the contentious direction is whether belief can be defined in terms of a threshold of degree of belief.
18 Some Bayesians might have an equally narrow conception of epistemology, on which neither knowledge or justified belief are properly epistemic, and full beliefs are not properly speaking the objects of epistemic evaluations. Instead, this conception of epistemology would have it that properly epistemic evaluations attribute to partial belief (a.k.a. credence) a limited menu of statuses: probabilistically coherent, properly updated in light of acquired evidence, and confirmed by evidence. This view is not so well-entrenched as the narrow conception I consider, so I will not consider it explicitly, here. The cases I consider in Chapter 4 will still, I think, be of interest to Bayesians, since they are apparently epistemic evaluations which seem not to be captured by that limited menu of statuses. Those cases concern (full) belief, but they could easily be adapted for partisans of partial beliefs.

their contents are propositional. Why deny that these are, in fact, the same sort of evaluation? Suppose that only one of S1 and S2 expresses a proposition, but that neither Abe nor Bea distinguish between S1 and S2 on that basis,[19] though Bea is good at spotting poor reasoning between sentences. If Abe then poorly reasons to S1 and to S2, then it seems to me that Bea could criticize the resulting cognitive states in the same way, despite only one of the two being a belief. So, if S2 happens to be the sentence which determines a proposition, and so the object of a belief, and the criticism of S2 is epistemic, then the criticism of Abe's non-belief attitude to S1 would also be epistemic.[20]

Similar problems afflict specific views of belief. Suppose that a therapist, or someone in therapy, explains their actions in terms of beliefs which they know to be false. On some views of belief, it can't actually be a *belief* that explains these actions, since belief aims at truth in such a way that it's impossible that S believes that p and knows that ~p. But we seem nonetheless to evaluate these cognitive states which fail to be beliefs in the same ways we evaluate beliefs: e.g. the "belief" which a patient knows to be false is irrational.

Besides this, we often seem to evaluate not simply a single specific cognitive state, but a vague collection or set of them, as when we say things like "his beliefs about aliens are unjustified," or "theoretical beliefs sustained since childhood are mostly unjustified." Perhaps these evaluations can be understood in terms of evaluations of individual beliefs, but it's certainly not obvious how. We might criticize a well educated scientist's religious beliefs in ways or to a degree that we wouldn't criticize the same beliefs in someone less well educated, even when the scientific beliefs do not seem to be evidentially relevant to the religious beliefs, so that with respect to each token belief, the two belief sets seem to be in rough justificatory parity. In that case, it looks like the significantly worse evaluation of the scientist's religious beliefs as a body can't be understood in terms of any of his beliefs being justificatorily worse than his less well educated counterpart. Nonetheless, the evaluations of collections of beliefs seem to be just as epistemic as the evaluation of particular beliefs.

In addition to these belief-like attitudes, we may evaluate propositional attitudes which are significantly less belief-like. For instance, we evaluate suppositions as incoherent, and we evaluate guesses as educated or good or bad. It is possible, of course, that an account could be given of these evaluations in terms of the badness of beliefs in the same contents. But that move is not available for non-propositional contents. And surely we can discriminate between better and worse guesses when the content of the guess does not succeed in expressing a proposition, just as we can discriminate between better and worse reasoning in such contents.

Moreover, it's not simply the *attitudes* which we evaluate in these ways. We also evaluate some contents. A self-refuting theory is bad for the same reason that a belief in it would be bad. Of course, a *disbelief* in a self-refuting theory may be epistemically good. But the point is just that we commonly evaluate theories themselves as good or bad, and might do so even if we denied that

---

[19] e.g. S1 = "the understanding of being in the *Aeneid* is completely different from the one in the *Oresteia*"; S2 = "the role of women in the *Aeneid* is completely different from the one in the *Oresteia*." Suppose for the sake of the example that S2 expresses a proposition, but S1 does not.

[20] This example assumes that we can make sense of reasoning between sentences. One might want to dispute that, and think in addition that there must be some beliefs – some propositional attitudes – standing behind our evaluations of Abe's non-belief attitude toward S1. An account of what reasoning between sentences comes to, and an argument that these evaluations cannot be explained by some propositional attitude that accompanies reasoning between sentences, would take us too far afield. My claim here is just that these are prima facie problems for the view that beliefs are the only proper subjects of epistemic evaluation.

there are any such things as beliefs. Besides, evidential support seems to make beliefs and the claims of a theory good in the same way: after all, evidential support is in the first instance a relation between *contents*, and only derivatively between attitudes to those contents. These all seem to me good prima facie reasons to think that some evaluations of sets of propositions and of theories are epistemic evaluations.

If theories are objects of epistemic evaluation, that is potentially very illuminating. For we evaluate theories not just for truth, or likelihood of truth, or evidential support, but for something else in addition, which Carnap tried to capture in terms of falsifiability, and some of his heirs in terms of informativeness.[21] One might also rate a theory for its contribution to understanding, for its explanatory power, elegance, and so on, where all of these seem independent of the likelihood that the theory is true. These seem like epistemic evaluations.[22] But they are factors which are left out, on the narrow conception of epistemology.

Even apart from non-propositional attitudes, and propositional contents rather than attitudes, we also seem to evaluate agents epistemically. If we say "Bea is rational," perhaps that means that Bea is generally disposed to have rational beliefs (in addition to being rational in other ways, e.g. making rational choices). It's hard to see why these would not count as epistemic, if what matters for the evaluation of the agent is other epistemic evaluations of beliefs. We also say things like "She's clever" or "he's crazy," which are not always so transparently connected to the status of beliefs. But if "Bea is rational" is an epistemic evaluation, it's hard to see why these other evaluations of agents aren't also epistemic.

III. Value and Value simpliciter

If values are just truthmakers for evaluations, then there are lots of values. When someone designs a game – chess, say – setting up rules and in particular determining what constitutes winning, a new body of evaluations comes into usage, e.g. "that was a good chess move." And these evaluations seem to be sometimes true. So, according to the account of value above, there is a kind of value – call it chess-value – which is either created or captured by the designer of the game.

But it would be strange to say that the designer of the game creates new values, or captures some pre-existing values. They could have come up with a completely different game. They could have even come up with anti-chess, with rules just like chess but where the object of the game is to lose. So anti-chess-value would be, in general, directly opposed to chess-value: good chess moves are bad anti-chess moves, and vice versa. How could both chess-value and anti-chess-value both be values?

Whatever values are, it seems strange to say that we can create or capture values that could be opposed in this way. But that seems to be a consequence of the present usage of "value," on which values are simply truthmakers for evaluations. In order to capture what is strange about the present usage, we might say that while chess-value is of value on the present usage, it is not of *real* value. Our evaluative practices are liberal, so that our willingness to evaluate things far exceeds our willingness to attribute value – that is, *real* value – to them.

Even more strangely, we can evaluate something *as a villain* or *for destructive potential*. But

---

[21] e.g. Huber 2008.
[22] I'm not claiming, here, that a less true (whatever that means) theory might be epistemically better; it would be enough for my point if informativeness (etc.) mattered for comparative judgements between equally true theories, e.g. that T1 is epistemically better than T2, although they're equally true, because T1 is more informative. That is the sort of role I propose for discursive epistemic value in Chapter 5.

there's something very unintuitive about saying that the truthmakers of "He's an excellent villain" or "the BH-2200 has outstanding destructive potential" are *values*. After all, isn't it bad to be a good villain, or to have great destructive potential? And if those are bad, then they seem to be disvalues rather than values. The valence of the evaluations is opposite to the valence of the real value; in these examples, the evaluations are positive, the real value negative. In addition to outstripping our willingness to attribute real value, our evaluative practices sometimes run counter to our intuitions about real value.

So something may be of value in the sense of being the truthmaker of an evaluation, but fail to be of real value. Now, there are many ways to try to capture the distinction between truthmakers for evaluations and real value. But what's of interest to me here is not the distinction itself or a particular way of capturing it, but rather the intuitions about real value themselves. For it seems to me that our intuitions about real value are unclear in one way that "knowledge is of value" is unclear. In particular, it's unclear whether, in order to be of value, something must make desires or preferences appropriate, or whether some things might be of real value because they make other attitudes appropriate. To see why, consider two opposing lines of thought about whether or not epistemic value is of real value.

On the one hand, epistemic value seems to matter for the status of one's *beliefs* in a special way – a way that chess value doesn't matter for the appropriateness of one's desires or beliefs or other attitudes. If a belief is epistemically bad,[23] then criticism of the belief is licensed. If a belief is epistemically good, then in some sense that is always a good thing: it *always* make that belief appropriate. But an action may be chess-wise bad, or a person may be good as a villain, although that isn't something that counts at all in favor of our desiring that the world include it. And although the action of performing a bad chess move is chess-wise bad, it may be that no criticism of the action is licensed, e.g. if nothing important hangs on the chess move, the player doesn't care about chess-value, the player's job depends on losing the game to his boss, and so on. So in one way epistemic value clearly does seem to be real value: epistemic value makes certain attitudes appropriate, viz. beliefs.

On the other hand, questions about value often seem to be questions about whether there would be something wrong with not *desiring* the thing of putative value, perhaps because questions of the form "what good is x" often seem to be roughly equivalent to questions of the form "what reason is there to want x?" Thus "what's the value of knowledge" can seem more or less equivalent to "what good is knowledge" and thus to "what reason is there to want knowledge?" And in this case, it's not clear whether knowledge, or anything else of epistemic value, is of real value.

So one reason that it's not clear whether epistemic value is of real value is that it's not clear whether real values are those that provide reasons for attitudes in general, or only those that provide reasons for desires. But since my interest here is in clarifying claims about epistemic value, rather than giving an account of intuitions about real value, I'll simply distinguish these two questions. Thus there are two ways we might understand the question we started with, "why is knowledge better than true belief?" The first question asks why, when we evaluate things epistemically, we criticize belief more than knowledge. That is, as I'll put it for brevity's sake, why is knowledge *epistemically* better than mere true belief? The second question, on the other hand, asks why we have reason to prefer knowledge to mere true belief.

This second kind of question, and the claims which would answer it, are about what I'll call

---

23 For "epistemically bad" here and elsewhere read: epistemically unjustified or otherwise of negative epistemic value, and similarly for "epistemically good," mutatis mutandis.

value simpliciter. Things that are of value simpliciter are things that there is reason to want.[24] A property is of value simpliciter iff for all S there is pro tanto reason for S to want things with that property. In particular, if epistemic goodness is of value simpliciter, then from the fact that something is epistemically good it follows that there is pro tanto reason for everyone to desire it. Consider the epistemic good of epistemic justification. Since epistemic justification is always an epistemic good, if epistemic goodness were of value simpliciter, it would follow that there is pro tanto reason for everyone to desire justified beliefs.

It matters quite a bit whether or not epistemic goodness is of value simpliciter. If it is, then the two questions distinguished above are likely to be answered together. That is because, in that case, knowledge is something there is reason to want if it is epistemically good, and it is epistemically good if it matters for the appropriateness of beliefs. So an understanding of one consideration – epistemic goodness – would at least partially answer both questions. Knowledge would be, at least in part, worth preferring to true belief *because* it is epistemically better.

On the other hand, if epistemic goodness is not of value simpliciter, then there will be an open question about any particular kind of epistemic goodness, namely: is there reason to want it? And if any particular kind of epistemic goodness is not of value simpliciter, then the equivalent question will be an open question for any token thing with that kind of epistemic goodness. If, for instance, justification is not of value simpliciter, then the mere fact that a belief is epistemically justified for S may not even provide a pro tanto reason for S to want the belief to be justified, although that fact provides a reason for S to believe it.

Perhaps because epistemic goodness is thought to be of value simpliciter, these two questions are not always kept separate, in the literature. For instance, consider a recent pair of articles by Kvanvig and David in *Contemporary Debates in Epistemology*,[25] which are ostensibly arguing for and against a single proposition: "truth is the primary epistemic goal."[26] David's argument is, very roughly, that we want justification for the sake of truth but not vice versa, so that, since justification and truth are the only two plausible candidates for a primary epistemic goal, truth must be it. Kvanvig, on the other hand, doesn't even consider, in his article, why anyone should desire justified beliefs. I suggest that the explanation for this disconnect is that Kvanvig is considering whether truth is primary in the account of how knowledge or justification matters for the appropriateness of beliefs, whereas David is considering whether truth is primary in the account of the reason to want justified beliefs. Kvanving is concerned with a question about specifically epistemic value, while David is concerned with a questions about value simpliciter.

IV. The Meno and Swamping Problems

Another place where it pays to distinguish the two questions is in trying to understand two specific problems – the swamping problem and the Meno problem – which often go together under the moniker of "the value problem."[27]

---

[24] This way of making the distinction, in terms of the kind of attitudes made appropriate, was suggested by Niko Kolodny. I employ it here for its relative clarity, but with a caveat. The caveat is that the real issue seems to me to be less determinate, namely whether the truth of "x is epistemically good" settles the truth of "x is good." And though "there is reason to desire x" is one relatively clear and more determinate way to understand "x is good," it's not obvious to me that it's the right way.
[25] Steup & Sosa 2005.
[26] Kvanvig 2005, David 2005.
[27] e.g. Pritchard 2010.

The Meno problem, as commonly formulated[28], is to explain why knowledge is of more value than mere true belief, given that they are equivalent for all practical purposes. On the other hand, the swamping problem is that, although truth seems to be in some sense the most important epistemic value, its primacy seems incompatible with knowledge being more epistemically valuable than mere true belief, since they are equally true – truth-wise equivalent, as we might say. So the swamping problem is posed by the truth-wise equivalence of knowledge and true belief, whereas the Meno problem is posed by their practical equivalence.

One way to understand the problems takes them to have the same explanandum, i.e. that knowledge is of more value than true belief, and treats each problem as placing different constraints on a single explanans, i.e. that it be consistent with both practical and truth-wise equivalence. On this understanding, the problem is adequately captured by the question "how can knowledge be of more value than true belief if they are both practically equivalent and truth-wise equivalent?" I suspect this is how most authors conceive of "the value problem."

But it's hard to see how the *practical* equivalence of knowledge and true belief could threaten to show that the two are equivalent as far as reasons for belief go. And it's hard to see how the truth-wise equivalence of knowledge and true belief would make a difference as far as reasons for desire go: in general, the truth-wise equivalence of two things doesn't entail equivalence of reasons to desire them. Leaving aside the possibility of those who can't handle the truth, there are also many things which are truth-wise equivalent because they are neither true nor false. Nonetheless, many of these truth-wise equivalent things are such that we should desire one but not the other. Happiness and wretchedness, for instance, are truth-wise equivalent. So it's hard to see what "value" could mean such that both practical equivalence and truth-wise equivalence appear incompatible with differences in value.

Nonetheless, we might justify treating the two problems together, if epistemic goodness were of value simpliciter. If we always and necessarily had pro tanto reason to desire epistemic goodness, then equivalence of pro tanto reasons to desire would entail equivalence of epistemic goodness. And in the other direction, equivalence of epistemic goodness would entail equivalence of pro tanto reasons to desire, ceteris paribus. So practical equivalence, by threatening equivalence of pro tanto reasons to prefer knowledge to true belief, would also threaten its epistemic betterness. And truth-wise equivalence, by threatening the epistemic betterness of knowledge, would also threaten pro tanto reasons to prefer it. But this would justify treating the two problems together only if epistemic goodness were of value simpliciter. And epistemic goodness is not of value simpliciter.

Epistemic goodness is not of value simpliciter

Is there pro tanto reason for everyone to want things that are epistemically good? For the sake of more concrete examples, let's consider the good of epistemic justification. Is there pro tanto reason for everyone to want justified beliefs? If not, then epistemic goodness is not of value simpliciter. In the first part of this section, I'll argue that the considerations usually cited do not show that epistemic justification is of value simpliciter. In the second part of this section, I'll argue that epistemic justification contributes to reasons to desire in a different way: it is not additive, as it would be if it were of value simpliciter, but rather ampliative. Epistemic value does not contribute to value simpliciter by always adding just a little bit – as a pro tanto reason would – but rather by strengthening other reasons we already have.

---

28   e.g. Pritchard 2012.

The usual considerations and their shortcomings
Justified beliefs seem in some sense likely to be true. If they are, then reasons to desire true beliefs will give us reasons to desire justified beliefs. So most of the debate over whether epistemic justification is of value simpliciter has been over whether we always have pro tanto reason to desire true beliefs. That is: for all agents S and true propositions p, is there pro tanto reason for S to desire to believe p?[29]

What I'll call the practical strategy argues that we have practical pro tanto reasons to desire true beliefs. In general, true beliefs contribute to successful action. Suppose I believe that the stairs are on the North side of the building, and I am right. That true belief will contribute to my success in escaping the building, in the event of a fire. If I had no belief, or if I had a false belief that the stairs were on the South side, those beliefs would not contribute to my success.

This strategy will only work, however, if *every* agent always has practical interests for which *every* true proposition matters. And this is a staggeringly strong claim. Surely there are proposition and subject pairs which are counterexamples to that. For instance, for most of us, the truth about the third entry under "Blackburn" in the 1976 Kansas City MO phonebook seems to matter not at all. In the same camp are astronomical trivia, like the number of protons in a certain quadrant near Alpha Centauri, and celebrity trivia, like the number of chihuahuas owned by A-list celebrities at midnight on Halloween in 2010. And of course there are many more kinds of trivia. What unites them all is their apparent remoteness from the practical interests of most people.

One strategy for circumventing this problem would expand the set of interests that matter. The idea is roughly that we have reason to promote others' interests, and others have interests which depend on the truth of trivia. The third "Blackburn" entry in the phonebook might be crucial to someone finding their birth parent, for instance. Someone might have made a bet on the number of chihuahuas. Someone else's astronomical theory might be falsified by the truth about the number of protons in that particular quadrant near Alpha Centauri. By lumping everyone's interests together, we can filter out the peculiarities of individuals' interests, such as apathy about trivia.[30]

Although this strategy will certainly broaden the range of propositions for which the explanation works, by including any proposition which matters for anyone, it won't solve the problem. Surely a more imaginative kind of trivia could escape even the practical interests of *some* actual people. For instance, disjunctive trivia about states of affairs radically different in content, and in radically different counterfactual situations: either the pope would wear an ecru hat made of unicorn leather, if unicorns were common, or there would have been no animals of a certain genus in Samoa, if Cantor had not come with the diagonal argument. So even if positing a common goal will help the practical strategy, it won't help *enough*: it won't show that epistemic justification is of value simpliciter.

Perhaps it is tempting to think that since "everything is connected," everything is potentially

---

29 This cannot be the *end* of the story about why we always have reason to desire justified beliefs, if there are some false justified beliefs. Presumably the thought is that I can never know that my belief that p is justified but false, since if I know that it's false, then it can't be justified for me. So, while there are some justified but false beliefs, we always have reason to desire justified beliefs because that is the best way we have to ensure that we have the true beliefs we want. I am not endorsing this line of thought – indeed, there seem to me to be serious problems with it – but I think something like this thought explains why arguments that justification is of value simpliciter have focused on the question whether true belief is of value simpliciter.
30 This strategy is suggested by Grimm 2009; the idea is developed (though not with reference to the concerns here) in Fallis 2007.

relevant to our practical interests. Even the propositions apparently most remote from our practical interests might, if false, have consequences we would care about. If there were so many protons in that particular quadrant near Alpha Centauri that a supernova was imminent, that fact would have catastrophic consequences for all of us.[31] If we came to know that the third "Blackburn" entry named JFK's assassin, then the truth about that third entry in the phonebook would matter to our practical interests.

One response would be to make the case that these counterfactual cases are not relevant to our practical interests. Of course, they *would* be relevant, if we were in those counterfactual circumstances. That's why they are potentially relevant to our practical interests. And they are potentially relevant to advice and deliberation, since we may not be able to rule out that those counterfactual circumstances are actual. But in the world as it is, this response would have it, they are not relevant to our practical interests.

This response would require significant development. Consider: we have reason to desire to believe the truth about the proposition "the destruction of the earth is imminent." But clearly there is some sense in which all astronomical trivia could be a difference maker for that truth. If the number of protons in any quadrant were high enough, for instance, perhaps that would make the imminent destruction of the earth significantly more likely. So if we understand "the truth of p matters for S's practical concerns" as "the truth value of p is a difference-maker for S's practical concerns," then it looks like trivia does matter for practical concerns after all. So, in order to discriminate between difference-makers which are actually relevant to our practical concerns, and those which are merely potentially relevant, we would at the very least need a different understanding of "the truth of p matters for S's practical concerns."

Fortunately, there is another reason to think that the practical strategy fails, which is considerably easier to make out. If there are some unverifiable truths, then those truths will not be difference-makers for anyone's practical concerns.[32] If there are some empirically adequate[33] falsehoods, then their negations will be truths that are not difference-makers for anyone's practical concerns. And surely there are both some unverifiable truths, and some empirically adequate falsehoods. So our practical interests do not give us reason to desire true beliefs for all propositions p.

So reasons for everyone to desire all true beliefs don't take root in our practical interests. Perhaps we might try to plant them instead in our curiosity. Isn't curiosity a natural desire to know or believe the truth? If it were, then everyone would have reason to desire true beliefs in order to promote the satisfaction of their curiosity. But surely that's not what curiosity is actually like – surely it is restricted to subject matter which is somehow important or interesting. Moreover, if that *were* what curiosity was like, then it would be dubious that any humans were curious.[34]

---

31 Thanks are due to John MacFarlane for pressing this worry.
32 Objection (pressed by John MacFarlane): suppose that you know you have a higher chance of succeeding at an unrepeatable task if some unverifiable truth, viz. p, is true than if p is false. Your success would not verify p. But p does matter for your practical concerns, if they include success at the unrepeatable task. Reply: your success would not verify p in the sense of conclusively verifying p. But surely your success would be *support* for p. So, contrary to the supposition, p would be verifiable after all. What the objection shows is that, by "unverifiable truths," we must mean "truths for which we can have no empirical support." The existence of truths for which we can have no *conclusive* empirical support would not suffice to make the point.
33 A claim, true or false, is empirically adequate "exactly if what it says about the observable things and events in the world is true" (Van Fraassen 1980, p. 12).
34 For more in depth consideration of curiosity, see Brady 2009.

Perhaps instead we should combine curiosity, as the source of reasons to desire true beliefs, with a very liberal conception of whose interests matter. If the curiosity of all possible cognizers matters to the common goal, and for each proposition there were a possible cognizer curious about that proposition, no matter how trivial or unverifiable,[35] then perhaps curiosity could give us an explanation of why we all have reason to desire true beliefs. And this explanation would encompass not only all trivia, but also those truths which are not difference-makers to anyone's practical interests. But this move would undermine the connection between true beliefs and something else that actual people ought to care about. For it is not the case that actual people ought to care about the curiosity of all possible cognizers. So neither curiosity nor our practical interests give everyone pro tanto reason to desire all true beliefs.

Kvanvig gives two different arguments that what he calls "pointless" truths[36] are prima facie good.[37] His idea, roughly, is that we should take truths without actual practical import – his "pointless truths" – to be of prima facie value which is *defeated*, rather than not to be of even prima facie value.

One argument Kvanvig gives for this is that otherwise we will not be able to account for why "basic research" is worthwhile. But surely "basic research" has plenty of less immediate, but wider-ranging, potential practical import. For instance, some pure math leads to the development of computers. Most basic research is an actually relevant difference-maker to our practical interests. If there are exceptions, they are in philosophy. And these cases would be prime candidates for being explained by curiosity. So this argument seems to me a nonstarter.

Kvanvig's better argument is that we do in fact have an intuition that supports the claim that we have pro tanto reason to desire true beliefs. The intuition is that god would be worse off if not omniscient. What defeats the value of many true beliefs for us, but not for god, is that many truths lack adequate informational content to justify cluttering up our finite intellects by adding beliefs in them.

Even if one has this intuition about god,[38] why treat reasons for *god* to desire something as probative for reasons for *us* to desire?[39] Presumably the idea is that the claim about god settles the prima facie goodness of true belief, so that it's a source of *pro tanto* reason for everyone. But what's the difference between being a pro tanto reason for everyone which happens to be defeated in all but one case, and being a reason only in that one case? And, perhaps more importantly, what would be diagnostic of that difference? It seems to me that there should be a strong presumption, in cases where something provides a reason for desire in only one case, to look for the source of that reason in something unique to the one case – say, in perfection, rather than in an attribute of god which we share in to a lesser degree. And if the source of the reason for god to desire true beliefs in pointless truths is perfection, then it clearly need not be the case that imperfect beings like us have reasons to desire beliefs in pointless truths.

---

35 Suggested, for instance, in Grimm 2009, p. 259 (emphasis mine): "This obligation stems... [from the fact that] any subject *might* come to have value ... in light of the varied and unpredictable concerns others *might* have."
36 Roughly, these are the truths in which we have no pro tanto practical or curiosity-based reason to desire beliefs.
37 Kvanvig 2008. I have preserved Kvanvig's use of "prima facie" here, though I take his point to be about pro tanto reasons, rather than things which seem prima facie to be pro tanto reasons, but might turn out not to be pro tanto reasons at all.
38 For a contrast, take Aristotle's divine substance, which has no knowledge of sensible particulars (it only has knowledge of any particulars if it is itself a particular).
39 What would it even mean for an omnipotent and eternally perfect being to have a reason to desire something?

If the point is supposed to be that any ideal cognitive agent will be omniscient in the sense of believing all truths, so that god is not the only relevant case, a deeper worry persists. We could grant that the cognitively ideal are *epistemically* better off than we are, while still wondering why we have any more reason to desire to be like them than we have to desire to be chess-masters or unsurpassable villains.

A simpler consideration which might show that we have pro tanto reason to desire true beliefs is that true belief seems choiceworthy. If given a choice between having or lacking a true belief on any proposition whatsoever, wouldn't you chose the true belief? What could explain this other than a pro tanto reason to desire true beliefs?
One explanation was hinted at in the introduction. This general fact about choiceworthiness might be underwritten not by the value of believing each truth, but by the overwhelming value of believing some small subset of truths – the secrets. So, in the same way that the expected utility of a bet may be positive although we are overwhelmingly unlikely to win, we might have reason to prefer a true belief to a false belief, all other things being equal. This is compatible not just with a lack of pro tanto reason to desire true beliefs in a majority of propositions, but with having a pro tanto reason to desire *not* to believe them.
We could rule out such explanations by comparing the choiceworthiness only of true and false *pointless* beliefs. If a pointless true belief, so described, still seems choiceworthy, this cannot be because of its greater expected utility. Would a pointless true belief still be choiceworthy?
There are really two questions here. One is what the *most* choiceworthy attitude is. And it seems clear that belief is not most choiceworthy: suspension is, for reasons of clutter-avoidance, if nothing else. The second question is whether belief would be better than disbelief. I suspect that most people have the intuition that they would prefer the true belief, though I find my intuition on this question wavers. But there is, I think, an undermining explanation of the intuition. When we have no reason to desire to have some type of thing, and are asked to choose between having a thing of that type which possesses some generally good property, and a thing of that type which has a property which is generally bad, we prefer the one which possesses some property which is generally good. And truth is a property we generally want our beliefs to have. So, if we must have beliefs in apparently pointless propositions, let them be true. This is, I think, even a rational heuristic: people often think truths are pointless which subsequently turn out to be very useful. Nonetheless, reasonable heuristics aside, it seems to me that an individual truth, if it is really pointless, is no more worthy of being believed than being disbelieved.
As long as the reason to prefer suspension of judgement in pointless truths seems to be a *practical* reason, there may be lingering intuitions that there is still *some* pro tanto reason to desire true beliefs – a distinctively epistemic or theoretical reason. I don't have an argument against this intuition. But I do think it's misplaced.
For one thing, I do think there is an intuition, which deserves to be taken seriously, that knowledge is always and necessarily epistemically better than mere true belief. And by failing to distinguish epistemic value from value simpliciter, we might end up confusing this intuition with the claim that knowledge is always and necessarily better simpliciter than mere true belief.
For another, it seems to me that the practical advantages of knowledge are systematically underappreciated by philosophers. Kvanvig's contrasts undergraduates who "prize knowledge only indirectly, in terms of what it can get for them in terms of money, prestige, power, and the like,"

with academics who "like to insist, instead, that knowledge is valuable for its own sake."[40] But surely we can instead make out this contrast in terms of those who prize knowledge for what it is very likely to get them in short-term, and academics who prize knowledge that is unlikely to result in any good to anyone any time soon – but might, of course, turn out to revolutionize society in the way that computers have. But both of these cases may involve reasons to desire knowledge which are rooted in our practical interests. Wanting knowledge for practical reasons need not make us crass.

On the account I offer in Chapter 2, there may well often be a specifically epistemic pro tanto reason to desire justified beliefs in propositions Kvanvig would classify as pointless. But that is *not* because there is a specifically epistemic pro tanto reason to desire *true* beliefs in pointless propositions.[41] Nor is it because there is always or necessarily a specifically epistemic pro tanto reason to desire justified beliefs.

There is sometimes no pro tanto reason to desire justified beliefs

Rather, it seems to me, justification is ampliative of the value of a belief, though properly value-neutral in itself. This is compatible with there being many token justified beliefs which there is pro tanto reason for everyone to desire: for instance, when they amplify the goodness of a good belief. But in the case of token beliefs for which justification amplifies their badness, there is pro tanto reason to desire not to have that justified belief. So epistemic justification is not of value simpliciter.[42]

These claims bear some unpacking. In particular, what does it mean for a property to be ampliative of the value of something else? And why think justification is ampliative?

The paradigm of an ampliative property is infectiousness, or a tendency to spread. Imagine two kinds of disease, both of which are fatal: one much more infectious than the other – perhaps one is spread only by blood transfusions, and the other causes and is spread by sneezing. Clearly the more infectious disease is the worse of these two.

But now suppose the disease resulted in a net benefit to the host, rather than in its death – for instance, take the beneficial bacteria of the human intestinal tract. Wouldn't their transmissibility make them better? If they weren't transmissible, then babies wouldn't get them from their mothers, and human digestion wouldn't work as well as it does.

In the case of infectious fatal diseases, transmissibility takes something which is generally bad, viz. a fatal disease, and makes it worse. In the case of transmissible beneficial gut bacteria, transmissibility takes something which is generally good, and makes it better. But there are also

---

40 Kvanvig 2003, p. 1.
41 Nor is it because there is *always* a specifically epistemic pro tanto reason to desire justified beliefs or knowledge, contrary to Sosa 2010, p. 188. Sosa's idea, in brief, is that in believing we are "endeavoring" to know, and that endeavoring to know entails a preference for knowledge. So when we ask ourselves if we would prefer knowledge rather than mere true belief, for instance, we notice our prior commitment to knowledge, and that prior commitment drives our intuition that knowledge is better. Two things to note: first, that this is an explanation of our preference for knowledge, not of a reason for that preference. Second, it is very hard to understand what it means to say that in believing *we* are endeavoring to do anything. Why does having a belief require taking on its aim, any more than having a dog requires marking one's territory?
42 Though I came to this thought independently, it is similar to a suggestion in Baehr 2009, p. 51: "It is plausible to think that for subject matters that are epistemically unworthy or disvaluable, we would do well (ceteris paribus) to devote as little of our cognitive capacity, as few of our resources, etc. as possible to such matters... If [this is] correct, then relative to many of the subject matters in question, knowledge is *less* valuable than mere true belief." Of course, I disagree with the suggestion that what matters to our reasons for desire is whether the subject matter is "epistemically unworthy." Sometimes we have excellent reason to desire to know tawdry secrets.

cases where transmissibility amplifies the value of a type where the tokens are neither generally good nor generally bad. Take, for example, the gene which codes for production of hemoglobin S. In some cases, producing hemoglobin S is good for an individual – it offers protection from malaria. But in cases where the gene is inherited from both parents and causes sickle-cell anemia, it is very bad for an individual. So, given that a transmissible gene for the production of hemoglobin S is better for many and much worse for a minority, is that gene good or bad? In this particular case, the answer to the question is not obvious. But if the gene is a good thing overall, surely it is better that it is transmissible, while if it is a bad thing overall, transmissibility makes it worse. So, again, transmissibility itself is neither good nor bad, but ampliative.

As a matter of empirical fact, justified beliefs are more likely to spread than unjustified beliefs. That is, if someone has a justified belief that p, that belief is more likely to be adopted by those who come into contact with them than an unjustified belief that p would be. Note that this is compatible with the existence of token unjustified beliefs that p which are more likely to be adopted than token justified beliefs that p. Justification is not all that matters to whether or not a belief is transmitted. But it is one thing that matters to whether or not beliefs are transmitted. This is why infectiousness might be a good model for the contribution justification makes to our reasons to desire.

Why think that infectiousness is a better model than the additive picture, on which justification always adds a pro tanto reason to desire justified beliefs? Both models predict that, ceteris paribus, we will have more reason to desire that our beliefs be justified, when we have reason to desire beliefs at all. Where they diverge will be on cases where we have reason to desire not to have beliefs. If justification is additive, we will still have reason to prefer justified beliefs to unjustified, in these cases. If justificiation is ampliative, we will have reason to instead prefer unjustified beliefs, in these cases.

Some cases of "positive illusions" show that justification is ampliative rather than additive. For instance, depressed subjects are typically less inaccurate when evaluating their own competence.[43] But this seems to be because non-depressed subjects routinely overrate their own competence, and the resulting inaccurate beliefs seem to be pragmatically good for the non-depressed – hence the name "positive illusions." Depressed subjects, on the other hand, have more accurate but debilitating beliefs about their own abilities.

Clearly, these debilitating beliefs can sometimes be well supported by evidence. Suppose that a depressed subject, Jane, is better able than others to succeed at some kind of task. Moreover, she has excellent evidence for her beliefs about her own abilities, including the belief that she can't perform a certain instance of that task. Jane is likely to transmit her justified beliefs about her own abilities (e.g. "I can't do it"). And this is likely to have the effect of making those around her doubt their own abilities, since they are less skilled than she is, and their beliefs that "Jane can't do it" are likely to be well supported by the evidence she is likely to relate to them. So the fact that her belief is justified is what enables it to spread; and that belief has bad effects for those who contract it.

In cases like this, of debilitating beliefs well supported by evidence, it looks as if everyone has pro tanto reason not to desire to have the belief, which happens to be justified, that Jane can't do it. And it looks like the justification of the belief only strengthens that pro tanto reason, rather than

---

43 For an overview of the psychological literature on depressive realism, see Alloy & Abramson 1988. For a recent philosophical take, see McKay & Dennett 2009. My point here, however, does not hang on the correct psychological account of actual human cognition.

providing a contrary pro tanto reason to desire belief.[44]

If that's right, then there is sometimes reason to desire epistemic justification, and sometimes not. So epistemic value is not of value simpliciter. And, if epistemic value is not of value simpliciter, then showing how knowledge is of more epistemic value than true belief despite being truth-wise equivalent will not show that knowledge is of more value simpliciter.[45] So solving the swamping problem won't, by itself, address the Meno problem. Nor will solving the Meno problem by itself address the swamping problem, since a story about why there is reason to prefer knowledge to true belief needn't show that it is preferable specifically because of its *epistemic* standing. The two problems need to be treated separately. I address the Meno problem, and the question of reasons to prefer epistemic goodness, in Chapter 2. In Chapter 3 I'll turn to the swamping problem, and the question of how to understand epistemic value.

Epistemic Oughts
The result that epistemic value is not of value simpliciter helps clear up another confusion, stemming from two different understandings of what "epistemic" contributes in claims about what we epistemically ought to believe. Reasoning from epistemic ought claims can result in an apparent tension between what people think is of epistemic value and the sort of beliefs they think people have reason to desire.

Take, for instance, a view of epistemic value commonly discussed:

(i) True beliefs are the only things of non-instrumental epistemic value

Suppose you believe (i), but you are persuaded by my earlier argument that

(ii) There is sometimes no pro tanto reason to desire true beliefs.

Then someone asks whether you agree or disagree that

(iii) One epistemically ought to have true beliefs.

But (iii) can look inconsistent with (ii). If you ought to be a certain way, then you must have reason to desire to be that way. That relationship to reasons to desire might seem to be constitutive of genuinely normative ought claims. And isn't epistemology genuinely normative?

On the other hand, (iii) seems to be entailed by (i). You epistemically ought to have things of epistemic value. And if, as (i) says, true beliefs are the only things of epistemic value, then surely you epistemically ought to have true beliefs. What else?

---

44 Though I developed this account independently, I have since discovered a close cousin of it in Steglich-Petersen 2011: "epistemic reasons to believe *that p* entail that one ought to believe that *p* only in the context of an all-things-considered reason to form a belief *about* p" (p. 15).

45 That is, showing that knowledge is of greater epistemic value would not *by itself* show that there is reason to desire knowledge. Scrupulous readers may worry that this example involving justification leaves open the possibility that knowledge has a different kind of epistemic value than justification. There is logical space for this view (though no one has yet occupied it, to my knowledge). But it seems to me that Jane's belief about her own abilities might well amount to knowledge. So the example seems to work, mutatis mutandis, for knowledge as well as for justification. So, for roughly the same reason that we do not have pro tanto reason to desire justification, we do not have pro tanto reason to desire knowledge.

So one might think that (i) and (ii) are inconsistent. I've argued for (ii), and will argue in Chapter 3 that (i) is false. But I do not think that (i) and (ii) are inconsistent. Rather, I think they seem inconsistent because of an ambiguity in (iii).

One way of reconciling these three claims would be to distinguish between subjective and objective senses of ought, and so hold that "ought" itself is here ambiguous.[46] Presumably, one would say that only the *objective* reading of (iii) is entailed by (i), but only the *subjective* reading of (iii) is in tension with (i).

Readers may, if they wish, reconcile these three claims by distinguishing in this way between different senses of "ought." But for my own part, I am not persuaded that ought is ambiguous in this way. Rather, I think that (iii) is ambiguous because the adverb "epistemically" can be read as making different contributions to the phrase "epistemically ought." Compare the different contributions "easily" and "hopefully" can make to similar phrases. If "he hopefully would," would he be hopeful? Would it be easy for her, if "she easily could?" I certainly do not think that "epistemically" in "epistemically ought" works just like "easily" and "hopefully." The point is just that the ambiguity of the phrases does not come from the ambiguity of the modal auxiliary.[47]

One way of understanding the contribution of "epistemically" takes "epistemic ought" claims to entail and be entailed by claims about value in the sense of values as truthmakers for epistemic evaluations. On this way of taking epistemic oughts, they are parallel to chess oughts. It seems to be true that one chess-wise ought to make the best chess move: to maximize chess-value. In the same way, it seems as if one epistemically ought to maximize epistemic value. One way to think of these claims is: if a certain kind of value is all that matters to S, then what would best satisfy S would be to maximize that kind of value. Another: from an epistemic perspective, maximizing epistemic value would be best (since that's all that matters), just as from a chess perspective, or if chess were all that mattered, maximizing chess value would be best. So (iii), understood in this way, is entailed by (i).

A view like Feldman's, on which "epistemic oughts" are like role oughts (e.g. "teachers ought to explain things clearly"), seems designed to capture these intuitions about epistemic oughts.[48] Likewise, when philosophers write things like "Abe epistemically ought to have true beliefs," that claim gets what plausibility it has from the claim that true beliefs are the only fundamental epistemic good, so what one ought to do from an epistemic perspective is to maximize the truth of one's belief.[49] But, again, this kind of ought claim doesn't entail that one has reason to desire true beliefs, just as chess oughts don't necessarily contribute to what one has reason to desire.

But on another way of understanding epistemic ought claims like (iii), they entail and are entailed by claims about what we have reason to desire, like (ii). On this second way of taking epistemic ought claims, if you are not as you epistemically ought to be, then you ought to want to be different. You ought to want to be a certain way, and your reasons for wanting to be that way are

---

46 There are other ways of making roughly the same distinction. Chisholm, for instance, uses a distinction from Braithwaite, between "practical" and "absolute" uses of ought (Chisholm 1957, p. 8).
47 In particular, I am agnostic as to whether "epistemically" is itself ambiguous, as "hopefully" is, or whether it has a unified semantics and scopes differently (modifying either the modal auxiliary itself, or its complement) in the two cases, as "easily" seems to.
48 Feldman 2000, p. 175.
49 There are other issues being swept under the carpet here for the sake of simplicity, e.g. that the relationship between epistemic value and epistemic oughts is not such that on this suggestion, one epistemically ought to acquire more true beliefs, but rather such that one epistemically ought to see to it that whatever beliefs one has are maximally true... i.e. true.

epistemic reasons. This is the sense that, for instance, Stephen Grimm wants to capture when he is trying to explain the more stringent way of being a normative discipline: if S's belief about grass is unjustified, "S should try to improve his cognitive position with respect to the grass, if possible."[50]

Since epistemic value is not of value simpliciter, this kind of epistemic ought doesn't entail that anything is of specifically epistemic value. Nor do claims about specifically epistemic values entail claims about what we have reason to desire. Since they are liable to be taken in these very different ways, and since none of the argument will turn on them, I will avoid epistemic ought claims in the rest of the dissertation.

V. The promise of virtue epistemology

Virtue epistemology is often supposed to hold special promise in solving "the value problem." But there are two very distinct problems virtue epistemologists have typically treated together. Which of these two problems is virtue epistemology supposed to promise to solve? The Meno problem, or the swamping problem?

The basic virtue-theoretic approach is to solve the problem by appealing to an Aristotelian distinction between doing the action a virtuous person would, and doing that action virtuously. And just as, in the case of actions, *doing an action virtuously* might be of more value than doing the same action but not virtuously, the idea in the case of beliefs is that knowledge is virtuous true belief, and having a virtuous true belief can be of more value than having a merely true belief. That is, knowledge has a kind of *praxical* value, according to Sosa's usage,[51] because it is "a kind of success through virtue,"[52] in Greco's phrase. The point of this value-theoretic move seems to be to explain how the value of a token justified belief is independent of the truth of that belief, because it is virtuous. The praxical value of knowledge will then be a matter not just of having true and virtuous beliefs, but of having beliefs that are true *because* virtuous.

This kind of praxical value – praxical epistemic value – is not of value simpliciter, if the argument of the previous section is correct. It's possible, of course, given what it means to be of value simpliciter, that some particular kind of epistemic betterness will turn out to be of value simpliciter, although epistemic betterness in general is not. But if the argument in the last section works at all, then it also works for praxical epistemic value. After all, Jane's belief was accurate and supported by evidence, and there is no reason it could not have been knowledge – no reason its accuracy couldn't have been *because* of its evidential support. So Jane's belief could have had praxical epistemic value; but we would still have had no reason to desire that belief or its praxical epistemic value.

For precisely this reason, it's hard to see how the virtue-theoretic move could help with the Meno problem. After all, one can point to the obvious greater *epistemic* value of knowledge, but that doesn't settle the question whether knowledge is of value simpliciter. That the greater epistemic value of knowledge happens to be praxical epistemic value is neither here nor there.

Moreover, if the point of introducing praxical value is to explain how the value of a token justified belief is independent of any facts about that belief other than its formation, it is hard to see how identifying the value of justified belief as *praxical* is going to license praise of the belief state

---

50 Grimm 2009, pp. 256-7.
51 Sosa 2003.
52 Greco 2009, p. 319.

itself, rather than, say, the method or process which resulted in the belief state, or the agent who formed the belief by using that method or process. So it's particularly hard to see why the belief itself, the bearer of praxical value, should be desirable on account of its praxical value.

Besides, there doesn't seem to be any reason why practical equivalence would have any less of a tendency to undercut the value of praxical epistemic value than plain old vanilla epistemic value. So, unless an account can be given of why, despite appearances, praxical epistemic value *is* less liable to be undercut by practical equivalence, it's hard to see why virtue epistemology is at an advantage in giving an answer to the Meno problem.

On the other hand, the praxical value of justified true beliefs looks more promising as an explanation of the swamping problem. Knowledge is no more true than true belief, but has more praxical value. This can seem like a solution to the swamping problem. So in Chapter 3 I'll return to virtue epistemology and consider whether it helps in solving the swamping problem.

VI. Epistemic Value and Naturalism

One source of interest in epistemic value is the desire to understand how epistemic values, like other values, fit with the rest of the world.[53] If the central contention of this chapter is right, this understanding is not well served by asking simply about "epistemic values" or "epistemic reasons," as many authors in the scholarly literature do. For instance, asking simply whether "epistemic reasons" have "categorical normative force"[54] papers over two different understandings of "epistemic reasons." Instead, if we want to understand metaphysical questions about epistemic value, we need to understand how epistemic value relates both to reasons to desire, and to reasons to believe. That is, we need to understand both what epistemic value is, and how it relates to value simpliciter.

I've argued against one initially plausible view about how epistemic value relates to reasons to believe. Epistemic value is not simply a kind of value simpliciter. There are some things of epistemic value which we do not have reason to desire. Since naturalists and moral skeptics deny that we have any reasons to desire other than, say, those grounded in natural facts or psychological facts, this result frees naturalists and skeptics from one burden they might be thought to bear. They need not give an account of why we have epistemic reasons to desire everything of epistemic value, regardless of what serves our interests or what we desire or value.

Of course, the naturalist or moral skeptic must still tell a plausible story about why we do have reason to desire things of epistemic value, when we do. And this story must be sensitive to what we value, or what serves our interests. In Chapter 2 I tell a story which, while it does not pretend to be complete, gives me hope for naturalism on this score.

However, on another front, naturalism and moral skepticism may not fare so well. For it does seem that epistemic reasons to believe are not sensitive in the right way to what we care about, or what serves our interests.[55] If my evidence does not support a belief in a pointless proposition, then my belief in that proposition would be epistemically bad. If my evidence strongly supported that belief, then my belief would be epistemically good. That is, of course, the point of saying that epistemic reasons have "categorical normative force."

---

53 For an early and explicit expression of just this motivation, see Lycan 1985.
54 As for instance, in Kelly 2003, pp. 616ff.
55 This is not to say that properly epistemic reasons are not sensitive in *any* way to our practical interests.

Now, it is not obvious that a naturalist or moral skeptic must give an account of the categorical normative force of reasons to believe. But since there is no space here to assess whether they must, suppose for purposes of the argument that they must. We could then ask whether a particular theory of epistemic value – of reasons for belief – was acceptable to a skeptic or naturalist.

The question whether a naturalist can give an adequate theory of epistemic value has attracted much attention recently, in large part because a naturalist account of epistemic value seems tied to the fate of a truth-monist account of epistemic value. The truth-monist account says, as I'll argue in Chapter 3, that all epistemic evaluations are explained by some relation the evaluated beliefs bear to their truth, and to their truth alone. This has seemed to some to be the only plausible and naturalistic account of epistemology. For the only other plausible account would put evidence in the place of fundamental explainer of epistemic value. And evidence only appears to be acceptable to a naturalist if they can give an account of evidence and evidential support on which it is a matter of standing in the right relation to truth. So evidential theories of epistemic value will either turn out to be truth-monist theories, or they will not be acceptable to a naturalist.

In Chapter 4 I'll develop two serious problems for truth-monist views of epistemic value. Epistemic value is not simply a matter of beliefs being likely to be true. Nor, I'll argue, is it simply a matter of having the right relation to one's own evidence. Thus the two most plausible truth-monist accounts are false.

The account I offer in Chapter 5 is not a truth-monist account, since it says that epistemic value is a matter of standing in the right relation not only to truth, but also to other cognizers. But this is an extension of truth-monism which is broadly friendly to naturalism. For it presents no new obstacle to naturalism, provided that cognizers can be understood as part of the natural world. Thus the fate of naturalism in epistemology is not tied as closely to truth-monism as it has been thought to be.

Chapter 2: The Meno Problem

The contemporary Meno problem takes its name and inspiration from a passage near the end of Plato's *Meno*, where Socrates brings up a problem for his earlier assumption[56] that knowledge is the only guide to correct action. The problem is that true belief seems to be no worse a guide to correct action than knowledge, so that knowledge is no more helpful than true belief: they are *practically equivalent*.[57] Meno initially resists, claiming that someone with knowledge will always meet with success, whereas someone with true belief will only succeed sometimes.[58] Socrates responds by reiterating the practical equivalence claim, but making some quantifiers explicit: someone who *always* has true belief will *always* succeed *so long as* she always opines truly.[59] This response overcomes Meno's initial resistance, but also makes him wonder: if the two are practically equivalent, why on earth do people value knowledge so much more highly than true belief?[60]

Meno's question seems to be a hard question precisely because knowledge seems to be of great practical value. But the practical equivalence to which Socrates points seems to show that this practical value can't be what makes knowledge *more* valuable than true belief. So one might wonder, with Meno: what does make knowledge better than true belief? This is the contemporary Meno problem: to explain why knowledge is better than true belief despite their practical equivalence.

My interest in this chapter is in the contemporary problem, rather than the problem as it arises in the *Meno*.[61] However, in order to understand the contemporary problem, it's going to be useful at several points to reflect on the *Meno*. In particular, I'm going to suggest that Socrates understands the threat of practical equivalence better than contemporary writers on it do, and proposes a very different solution to it than they do. Contemporary authors often suppose that a

---

56 at 88a-e, where "knowledge" is used seemingly interchangeably with "wisdom" and several more involved cognitive blandishments.
57 97b5-7 gives the quantified token-level claim about leading: "And I suppose, so long as he has correct opinion about what the other one has knowledge of, he will be in no way a worse guide, thinking the truth, but not knowing it, than the knower" ("Καὶ ἕως γ' ἂν που ὀρθὴν δόξαν ἔχῃ περὶ ὧν ὁ ἕτερος ἐπιστήμην, οὐδὲν χείρων ἡγεμὼν ἔσται, οἰόμενος μὲν ἀληθῆ, φρονῶν δὲ μή, τοῦ τοῦτο φρονοῦντος). The conclusion about true belief as a leader is drawn at 97b9-10: "So true opinion is in no way a worse guide to correct action than knowledge" (Δόξα ἄρα ἀληθὴς πρὸς ὀρθότητα πράξεως οὐδὲν χείρων ἡγεμὼν φρονήσεως). And these facts about leading are immediately taken to show that knowledge is no more *helpful* than true belief, or at any rate, ὀρθὴ δόξα at 97c4-5: "So in no way is true belief less helpful than knowledge" (Οὐδὲν ἄρα ἧττον ὠφέλιμόν ἐστιν ὀρθὴ δόξα ἐπιστήμης). The shift here to ὀρθὴ δόξα is potentially significant – it might be read as 'the right belief' rather than 'true belief' – and persists to 97e6. But I'll treat it here as mere variatio without significance, for the sake of getting clear on one set of issues.
58 97c6-8: "To this degree, Socrates, that the one with knowledge will always succeed, while the one with correct opinion will succeed sometimes, and sometimes will not." (Τοσούτῳ γε, ὦ Σώκρατες, ὅτι ὁ μὲν τὴν ἐπιστήμην ἔχων ἀεὶ ἂν ἐπιτυγχάνοι, ὁ δὲ τὴν ὀρθὴν δόξαν τοτὲ μὲν ἂν τυγχάνοι, τοτὲ δ' οὔ).
59 97c9-10: "Will someone who always has correct opinion not always succeed, so long as he opines correctly?" (ὁ ἀεὶ ἔχων ὀρθὴν δόξαν οὐκ ἀεὶ ἂν τυγχάνοι, ἕωσπερ ὀρθὰ δοξάζοι;).
60 97c11-d2: "I wonder, Socrates, this being so, why on earth knowledge is much more prized than correct opinion." (θαυμάζω, ὦ Σώκρατες, τούτου οὕτως ἔχοντος, ὅτι δή ποτε πολὺ τιμωτέρα ἡ ἐπιστήμη τῆς ὀρθῆς δόξης).
61 In two other papers, I defend the relevant interpretive claims about the *Meno*. In *Knowledge is Teachable*, I argue that this answer which in this paper I attribute to Socrates is at least in the background of the *Meno*. In *The Stability of Knowledge*, I argue that we should understand stability – Socrates' official answer to Meno's question – along the same lines.

solution to Meno's challenge will cite some non-practical value that knowledge has. In contrast, the Socratic solution I will champion is resolutely practical.

There are other practical solutions to the problem. In the introduction, I briefly discussed what I there called a *content*-driven solution, which paints the epistemic status of knowledge as a by-product of the kind of investigation which is most efficient at discovering secrets. But there are straightforward reasons to be dissatisfied with this solution, since there is something very misleading about saying that a byproduct is valuable. It may be associated with a valuable state of affairs, but it is not what makes the valuable state of affairs valuable.

A more satisfying practical solution has been recently defended by Williamson and Fricker: that knowledge makes future true belief more likely.[62] Thus knowledge is better than true belief because of its effects over the course of time. I do not find this solution wholly satisfying. For one thing, I have the intuition that knowledge would be preferable to true belief even in situations where neither will have any future effects, say because death or the end of the world is imminent. But there is also a deeper reason for dissatisfaction with this practical solution, which will become clear in the course of the chapter.

Although many commentators think that Socrates is expressing just this practical solution, when he responds to Meno's question by saying that knowledge is stable,[63] I take "stable" to instead express a better answer Socrates gives more explicitly earlier in the *Meno*: that knowledge is teachable. This is also a practical solution to the Meno problem, since our reasons to desire an ability to teach are practical reasons. But it is a better practical solution than a close relation which can be found in the literature, on which knowledge makes one more likely to be able to persuade others.[64]

These practical solutions, however, have not been widely accepted, for two reasons. One is simply that commentators often seem to think that knowledge in general has *no* practical advantage over true belief. Thus Kvanvig says that "true opinion … is equally useful, and yet knowledge is more valuable than true opinion. Hence the value of knowledge must be explained in terms beyond its pragmatic usefulness."[65] And Sosa says that, if you are trying to go to Larissa, "a true belief will get you there just as well."[66] But this is false, for reasons that will become clear later in this chapter.

The other reason practical solutions have been thought inadequate is that it has been thought that the Meno problem requires an explanation which holds in every possible situation. And there is no practical solution which holds in every possible situation. There is not always practical reason to

---

62 Williamson 2000 (see esp. p. 79) and Fricker 2007.
63 e.g. Scott 2006 p. 180, fn. 7:"In the Meno, the point is that someone who merely believes that p is likely to stop believing it in favor of not-p."
64 Jones 1997 explicitly puts forward a solution in terms of persuasion, which is itself inspired in part by Craig 1999.
65 Kvanvig 2003, p. 4.
66 Sosa 2010, p. 167. It is not clear that Sosa thinks the point generalizes, since he later restates the point: "Nor is knowledge necessarily better as a means to our relevant objectives. This is the point made in the *Meno*. Some true means-ends beliefs will help us to attain our ends just as well as knowledge." Sosa's footnote to this clarification criticizes the answer Williamson and Fricker give, so it looks as if Sosa intends to be saying not just that there are some circumstances where a true means-ends belief will help us to attain our ends just as well as knowledge, but also that there are some true means-ends beliefs which are just as good as knowledge, whatever the circumstances. If so, that seems very unlikely. Surely for any means-end belief, there are some circumstances which might befuddle a mere true believer, but where a knower would persist. In any event, if this is not Sosa's response to Williamson, it is unclear how he would respond.

prefer knowledge to true belief. So, if the problem is to explain why knowledge is always preferable to true belief, there will be no practical solution to the problem. But, as I argued in Chapter 1, knowledge is not always preferable to true belief. So this is no inadequacy of practical solutions.

Unless the problem is simply insoluble, the problem cannot be to explain why knowledge is preferable to true belief in every possible situation, or even in any actual situation. But if that is not the problem, what is? What does it mean, here, to say that "knowledge is better than true belief?" And how should we understand the quantifiers implicit in that explanandum, if not as universal quantifiers, saying that knowledge is in every possible situation better than true belief? Equally importantly, what does Socrates' practical equivalence claim mean, and how exactly does if figure in the Meno problem? In the next section of the chapter, I try to get clearer on each of these questions.

I. Understanding the Meno Problem

Quantifiers

It's difficult to understand exactly how to quantify the explanandum, but the *Meno* is a helpful model, here. Meno's worry isn't about some exceptions to the general rule that knowledge is of more value. Rather, his worry is that the general rule is wrong. He's wondering why people *ever* value knowledge, or why they *usually* value it as highly as they do – not why they always, everywhere, and necessarily value it.

In this respect, Meno's question is like many everyday questions of the form "what good is x?" Such questions often neither require nor admit of exceptionless or universal answers, although they do require systematic answers. Why is artisanal bread better than non-artisanal bread? There is a sense in which "because it is tastier" is a better answer than less systematic answers. But there is no exceptionless or necessary answer to the question at all. Not all artisanal bread is tastier. Similarly, what good is a car? "A car makes some kinds of transportation easier" seems like a good answer, even though a car doesn't make transportation any easier when it's broken, or when traffic is bad, or when you have to cross an ocean to get to your destination. Like these two questions, Meno's question is a layman's question. And insofar as the Meno problem is a problem, it seems to me, it is a problem that involves a layman's question about value, rather than a question about the value any bit of knowledge would have in any possible situation.

The generality of the layman's question explains one thing that would be unsatisfying about content-driven explanations of the value of knowledge. If knowledge in general were of value because of the overwhelming value of a relatively small percentage of knowledge – the secrets, as the content-driven explanation in the introduction had it – then the appropriate answer to Meno's question would be that it's not *knowledge* that is better than mere true belief. In that case, knowledge would be like lottery tickets. Compare: what good are lottery tickets? They're certainly not like checks, though neither of them is redeemable for cash in every possible situation. A more systematic connection between knowledge and practical benefit is required of an answer to Meno's question, and so, I suggest, is also required of a solution to the Meno problem.

This generality need not hold in all possible worlds, however. Suppose that a militantly fideistic deity punishes those who know things, but not those who merely truly believe them. Kvanvig takes such demon-worlds to be relevant to solving the Meno problem, since he takes them to rule out Williamson's practical solution.[67] It's clear that, in that demon-world, knowledge would not have the practical value that it does in this world. But it also seems clear that this is compatible with knowledge having more practical value in this world.

I doubt that the problem of understanding these layman's value claims can be assimilated to the problem of understanding generic quantifiers, even if they are often expressed in the same way: "in general, dogs have four legs" is not sensitive to facts about the utterer's and hearer's circumstances that value claims will be. For instance, it is often thought that the generic "in general, dogs have four legs" would be true in circumstances in which a majority of dogs did not in fact have four legs. But in such a world (or in a particularly three-legged corner of it) "in general, dogs are good sled-pullers" might well not be true, and so neither would "in general, S has reason to desire dogs" be true for those S who have reason to desire that their sleds be pulled. The problem seems to be that these value claims are tied to advice in a way that other generics are not.

I don't have an account to give or adopt, here, of how to quantify the claim Meno wants an explanation of. But in order to have a way to discuss that claim, I'll use the quantifier "in general," as in "Meno wants to know why, in general, knowledge is better than true belief." What matters most for understanding the Meno problem is simply that we not demand an exceptionless answer, or one that holds, even for the most part, in all possible worlds.

"knowledge is better than mere true belief"

What does it mean to say that knowledge is better than mere true belief? There's a way of hearing that claim as almost trivially true, and not in need of explanation. After all, one might think, to call something knowledge is to evaluate it positively in one way – epistemically. And along with these positive evaluations, when they're true, comes a special kind of value: epistemic value. That's a way in which knowledge is clearly better than true belief: it's of more *epistemic* value.

Even if it weren't clear that knowledge is of more epistemic value than mere true belief, it's hard to see how practical equivalence could cast doubt on the greater epistemic value of knowledge. Pragmatic reasons for belief don't make beliefs *epistemically* good. And just as pragmatic *in*equivalence doesn't matter to whether one thing has more epistemic value than another, so pragmatic equivalence doesn't threaten any plausible explanations of why knowledge is of greater *epistemic* value than true belief.[68] Lack of pragmatic value would be a result of no significance for a claim about epistemic value.

So, if this were the right way to understand Meno's wonder – if, that is, the explanandum were a claim about *epistemic* value, then the Meno problem could only be that Meno is blind to epistemic value, in more or less the same way that blindness to aesthetic value might lead someone to wonder why people prize Cézanne paintings over paintings by Thomas Kinkade, painter of light.[69]

---

67 Kvanvig 2003, p. 17.
68 I take it that proponents of "pragmatic encroachment" (e.g. Fantl & McGrath 2002, Hawthorne 2004, Stanley 2005) are developing views about the semantics of terms which epistemology traditionally deals with, like "epistemically justified" or "knows." But I don't take those proponents to be putting forward theses on which pragmatic reasons for belief are difference-makers to properly epistemic evaluations, as opposed to pragmatic features of apparently epistemic evaluations which, if they are right, turn out to be a kind of hybrid evaluation, like saying "his belief is epistemically bad, but in this case it doesn't matter much." That is not to say that proponents of pragmatic encroachment would agree with this description of their positions. But although they may think that pragmatic reasons do sometimes make a difference to epistemic evaluations, they should admit that pragmatic equivalence does not threaten a plausible answer to Meno's question. After all, they don't claim that *only* pragmatic features make a difference to epistemic value.
69 Controlling, of course, for the fact that Cézanne painting are worth much more money. If you prefer, take the

It is possible to make out *a* problem along these lines, on which we who recognize that knowledge has greater epistemic value than mere true belief might try to make that value salient to Meno, in more or less the same way that we might try to make the greater aesthetic value of the Cézanne salient to someone. But the problem on this understanding of the explanandum would, to put it crudely, be Meno's problem, rather than a problem for plausible explanations of the value of knowledge. Moreover, practical equivalence would be relevant at most as the cause of Meno's blindness, rather than as a reason for his wonder. So, while blindness to epistemic value is *a* problem, a better name for it might be "the humanities' funding problem" - and that, at any rate, is not the Meno problem.[70]

But there are other ways to take the explanandum on which it is not about specifically epistemic value, as I pointed out in Chapter 1. Suppose Meno had wondered why people prize good chess moves more highly than bad ones. Of course, he recognizes that good chess moves are good chess moves – they have, as it were, positive chess value. So the issue is not whether a certain body of evaluative practice is right – whether the moves we usually evaluate as good chess moves really are good chess moves. His question is external to that body of evaluative practices. In the same way, Meno's question about knowledge is not whether knowledge is of more *epistemic* value than mere true belief. His question is external to the practice of evaluating things as epistemically good or epistemically bad.

One clear way to make out this external question is in terms of reasons for preferences: what reason is there to prefer good chess moves to bad chess moves, or to prefer knowledge rather than mere true belief?[71] On this understanding of Meno's question, practical equivalence is at least a prima facie problem, as it is supposed to be. Practical equivalence would rule out one common and powerful kind of reason to prefer knowledge to mere true belief: practical reasons. So the best way to take "knowledge is of more value than true belief" is as a claim about reasons to prefer knowledge to mere true belief. Thus the problem appears to be to find an explanation of what I'll call the "Meno Problem Explanandum"

(MPE) In general, cognizer S has reason to prefer knowing p to merely truly believing p.

In the interest of brevity, I'll often just say "knowledge is more valuable than true belief" in the rest of the chapter, but throughout I'll take that to be a claim about what, in general, agents have

---

comparison to be between the most expensive pieces by Rodin and by Damien Hirst, which are roughly financial equivalents (Hirst: $19,213,270; Rodin $18,969,000 – cf.
http://www.askart.com/AskART/interest/top_artists.aspx?interest=AskARTTopAuctionPrices&id=27)

70 There is a closely related problem for specifically epistemic value, viz. the swamping problem. My point here is just that practical equivalence doesn't pose a threat to the specifically epistemic value of knowledge. In contrast, the swamping problem takes the status of truth as the only basic epistemic value to make problematic how knowledge can be of more epistemic value than mere true belief.

71 In fact, I think Meno's question is less determinate, and that there may be answers to it which would not cite reasons to prefer knowledge to true belief, so long as they show that knowledge is *better*, full stop, rather than just *epistemically* better. For instance, perhaps Meno is neglecting a natural human curiosity which knowledge but not mere true belief fulfills, and which is a desire all humans happen to have although it's not the case that they have reason to have the desire. As an empirical claim, that seems pretty unlikely – but the present point is just that some such answers are possible, and I am not intending by this formulation to rule them out. Nevertheless, for the sake of clarity, and in order to avoid disputes about the semantics of claims about goodness *simpliciter*, I will ignore those possible answers here.

reason to prefer.

Although the problem is put in terms of knowledge, it's clear that we could ask similar questions about other epistemic statuses. Knowledge is not the only epistemic status threatened by practical equivalence. We might also wonder, for instance, why we have reason to prefer justified true beliefs, or beliefs which are supported by evidence, but not so well supported that they amount to knowledge. For that matter, we might wonder whether we have reason to prefer justified false beliefs to unjustified false beliefs. It seems quite plausible that in general we do.[72] For instance, we have reason to prefer that scientists have justified beliefs rather than unjustified beliefs, even though their theoretical beliefs seem likely to be false.[73] And we might wonder not just about justification and evidential support, but about other apparently epistemic statuses people have discussed. We might ask whether we have reason to prefer understanding to a lack of understanding, and if so why we do. After all, wouldn't a GPS, which lacks any understanding at all, be just as good a guide to Larissa as someone with understanding of the road to Larissa (supposing, of course, that such a thing is a possible object of understanding). Why should we prefer understanding to having a GPS, at least for directions? So the Meno problem seems to generalize from knowledge to other epistemic statuses.

It is for this reason that explanations of MPE in terms of justification are unsatisfying. Simply asserting that, in general, we have reason to desire that our beliefs be justified, would not answer Meno's question. Of course, on the account that I will offer, we do often have reason to desire justification. But the account I'll offer explains *why* we have reason to desire justification.

In addition, since the Meno problem generalizes from knowledge to other epistemic statuses, it is tempting to think that the basic problem is to explain why, in general, we have reason to prefer things of greater epistemic value to things of lesser epistemic value. Although I think that that claim is true, an adequate assessment of it requires a more complete and precise account of epistemic value than I aim to give in this dissertation. So I will rest content with a more modest claim, here: the account later in this chapter of our reasons to desire things of epistemic value coheres well with the picture of epistemic value I paint in Chapter 5. We have reasons to prefer discursive abilities, and discursive abilities come with discursive epistemic value.

The structure of the problem

For the moment, though, I'll focus on knowledge, and so on MPE. One natural way to

---

72 Perhaps the case of *false* beliefs is disanalogous, since in this case our preferences for justified beliefs might be our preferences are made rational by the fact that the justified beliefs are in some sense more likely to be true. By contrast, a greater likelihood of truth seems not to give us reason to prefer knowledge or justified true belief to mere true belief. Do we have reason to prefer to bet on a horse that is likely to win a race? Yes, if the alternative is a bet on a horse that is less likely to win, ceteris paribus. But do we have reason to prefer a bet on a horse that is likely to win to a bet on a horse that *will* win? So it looks implausible that our reasons to prefer beliefs which are likely to be true gives us reason to prefer either justified true belief or knowledge to mere true belief. This is the analogue, for reasons to prefer, of the swamping problem, to be discussed in Chapter 3, which is about reasons to prefer knowledge to true belief. To be clear: I do not think this is anything like a conclusive objection to the claim that in general we have reason to prefer beliefs that are likely to be true, and that this gives us reason to prefer justified true beliefs to unjustified true beliefs, or knowledge to mere true belief. But I do find the objection plausible enough to postpone what would be a lengthy evaluation of its force.

73 Note that I am not taking a stand on the pessimistic induction which says that most scientific theories are false, therefore our present scientific theories are probably false (see, e.g., Laudan 1981). The point here is that judgements (or at least my judgements) about the choiceworthiness of justified false beliefs over unjustified false beliefs is not sensitive to whether I think the scientists' beliefs are true. I think most people retain the judgement even when they accept the conclusion of the pessimistic induction.

understand the structure of the problem takes the practical equivalence claim to be a constraint on potential explanations of MPE. On this conception of the problem, practical equivalence is inconsistent with some plausible explanations of MPE, for instance that we generally have practical reason to prefer knowledge. To solve the problem is just to find some explanation of MPE which is consistent with practical equivalence.

Practical equivalence

In order to understand the problem in this way, we'll have to get clearer on the practical equivalence claim. In what sense does Socrates think that knowledge and belief will be practically equivalent? Recall his reformulation of it: "Won't the one who always has correct opinion always hit the mark, so long as he opines correctly?"[74] Assuming that "hitting the mark" just means performing the same successful actions as the person with knowledge, the thought seems to be that knowledge and true belief will result in the same successful actions.[75] But what this means, of course, depends on what each "always" is doing in Socrates' formulation.

A first, very naïve, pass at understanding and precisely formulating practical equivalence might be: someone who knows p will perform the same actions as someone who merely truly believes p. That is:

(PE1) $(p)(\varphi)(S,S')$. (S knows p & S' merely truly believes p) → (S will φ ≡ S' will φ)[76]

The problem with this formulation of practical equivalence, of course, is that it's obviously false, since it doesn't restrict at all the motivational set or background cognitive states of S and S'. If, for instance, Knut (the knower) knows that the middle road leads to Larissa, and Trudy (the mere true believer) merely truly believes that, but Knut wants to mislead you and Trudy doesn't, then Trudy is far more likely to lead you to Larissa. Even if S and S' have the same motivational set, they may significantly differ in their background cognitive state. For instance, if Knut believes that Larissa is currently being sacked by the Persians, and Trudy does not, then although in some sense they might be equally good guides to Larissa, Knut would be far less likely to actually guide one there.

One way to capture the practical equivalence claim would be to replace the antecedent of PE1 with "S and S' share the *relevant* motivational and background cognitive set." Indeed, it seems likely that this is how most commentators have conceived of the problem. But without a precise account of which beliefs are relevant, this isn't going to be illuminating.

A way to avoid the obvious falsity of PE1 while retaining its precision would be revise the antecedent to rule out differences in action due to differences in background cognitive or motivation

---

74   97c9-10: ὁ ἀεὶ ἔχων ὀρθὴν δόξαν οὐκ ἀεὶ ἂν τυγχάνοι, ἕωσπερ ὀρθὰ δοξάζοι;

75   This is an assumption for the purpose of simplifying the presentation; in fact, as it will turn out, I think that knowledge and true belief don't always result in the same successful actions. But I don't think that worries about the individuation of *actions* are going to provide a satisfying answer to Meno's question. Suppose, for instance, that we individuate actions so that the virtuous person who helps an old lady across the street actually performs a different action from the non-virtuous person who helps an old lady across the street. It's hard to see why Meno should have any preference as to whether to perform one of these actions rather than the other.

76   p ranges over all propositions, φ ranges over potential actions, and S and S' over agents. One might think that practical equivalence should include some explanatory language, e.g. by replacing "S will φ" with "S will φ because of knowing p," and similarly "S' will φ because of truly believing p." I leave causal language out, for simplicity's sake, since it won't help with the problem I want to bring out: the difficulty of making out exactly what other beliefs count as *relevant*.

state. The clearest way to do that would give us this second practical equivalence claim: two people who are *exactly* alike, both cognitively and motivationally, except that one knows p, and the other merely truly believes it, will perform the same actions. That is,

(PE2) (p)(φ)(S,S').(S & S' have same motivational set & same cognitive state except w.r.t. p[77])→
(S will φ ≡ S' will φ)

But PE2 doesn't generate a very hard problem. For although it seems plausibe, and perhaps rules out *some* plausible explanation of the practical benefits of knowledge, it nevertheless paves the way for a very plausible explanation of MPE. For if someone knows that p, they are more likely to know and thus have true beliefs about other things related to p, such as things that presuppose p, the conclusions of arguments in which p figures as a premise, and others of what I'll call p's kin,[78] than if they merely truly believe p. The person who knows how to get to Larissa is more likely to know, and so have true beliefs about, for instance, how to get to points past Larissa. That is consistent with PE2, and seems to explain MPE. Does it solve the problem?

Surely not. While PE2 might give rise to one easily solved version of the Meno problem, the antecedent in PE2 is too strong to capture the hardest version of the problem, since it compares virtual mental duplicates, of which there are none in the actual world. So it's no wonder that PE2 is not incompatible with explanations of the value of knowledge over mere true belief in normal circumstances – i.e. explanations of MPE. But, for the same reason, this surely doesn't capture Meno's worry.

One way to weaken the antecedent would be to allow S' to be cognitively just like S except that S will know, and S' merely truly believe, not just p but all p's kin. And perhaps that's even intended to be the force of the first "always" in Socrates' claim: for each bit of knowledge which S has, S' has true beliefs. That gives us a third practical equivalence claim: two people who are exactly alike, both cognitively and motivationally, except that one knows p *and its kin*, and the other merely truly believes p *and its kin*, will perform the same actions. That is:

(PE3) (p)(φ)(S,S'). (S & S' have same motivational set, same cognitive state except w.r.t {p & kin})→
(S will φ ≡ S' will φ)

If PE3 were true, then it would rule out an explanation of MPE in terms of S now having true beliefs in p's kin, since it says that anyone who has those other true beliefs will perform the same actions as someone who knows them. But, like PE1, PE3 is clearly false.[79] The cognitive associates of a knowledge state are not limited to a single moment in time; they're also spread across time. So even if S and S' satisfy the antecedent of PE3, S and S' may perform different actions in the future because S *will have* true beliefs when S' will not. For instance, in Williamson's example,[80] a

---

[77] w.r.t. = "with respect to." That is, S and S' have the same motivational set, and the same cognitive state except that S knows p and S' merely truly believes p.

[78] This gloss is just intended to acknowledge that there are many other ways in which knowing p is a predictor of knowing other things which are in some way like p: for instance if one came to know p by means m, then one is more likely to know other things by m than is someone who merely truly believes p. If one sees the writing on the wall, one is ceteris paribus more likely to see the picture on the wall; if one knows which cars one's co-workers drive, one is ceteris paribus more likely to know when they go on vacation; and so on.

[79] PE2 will be false for the same reason, of course.

[80] Williamson 2000, pp. 62-63.

diamond thief who *knows* that there is a diamond in the bedroom will persevere in situations where many mere true believers would give up. For that reason, if Knut knows that the diamond is in the bedroom, Knut would make a better diamond-thief than Trudy. Since clearly false principles pose no problem in explaining anything, it can't be PE3 which is problematic.

One way to weaken PE3 would be by taking Socrates' "always" more literally, and adding a temporal quantifier to its antecedent, so that we will only consider agents who not only don't now differ in true beliefs with respect to p and its kin, but who *never* so differ. That gives us a fourth practical equivalence claim: two people who are *always* exactly alike, both cognitively and motivationally, except that one now knows p and its kin, and the other now merely truly believes p and its kin, will perform the same actions. That is,

(PE4) $(p)(\varphi)(S,S')$. (S & S' *always* have same motivational & cognitive state except w.r.t {p & kin}) → (S will $\varphi \equiv$ S' will φ)

PE4 is at least plausibly true. But now it looks like we can explain MPE, despite PE4, by reference to the very facts which motivated it, about the cognitive effects of knowledge across time. Even if knowledge doesn't have different cognitive effects across time *for S and S'*, it is still true that knowledge does have different cognitive effects over time in normal circumstances. The problem with S and S' is that they aren't in normal circumstances: in fact, they're in very peculiar and unlikely circumstances. And so the different cognitive effects of knowing over time are consistent with PE4, and seem to explain MPE.

This explanation is precisely the practical solution to the Meno problem which Williamson and Fricker favor. In Williamson's formulation: "If your cognitive faculties are in good order, the probability of your believing p tomorrow is greater conditional on your knowing p today than on your merely believing p truly today (that is, believing p truly without knowing p)."[81]

One might worry that Williamson's claim here is just in terms of future belief, with no mention of the belief's truth.[82] And surely it's not the higher likelihood of future belief which matters most to solving Meno's problem, but the higher likelihood of future *true* belief.[83] After all, it's only if knowledge makes future *true* belief more likely, that we can explain why knowledge is better than true belief in terms of knowledge having *more* of whatever makes *true* belief good, for instance in terms of the greater likelihood of successful actions which come with true beliefs. So this gives us an explanation for MPE which is consistent with all of the practical equivalence claims so far formulated. Someone who knows p is more likely to have a future true belief that p than someone who merely truly believes p. I'll call this FTB – the "future true belief" explanation:

(FTB) $(s)(p).(\Pr(sTBp \text{ in the future } | sKp) > \Pr(sTBp \text{ in the future } | sTBp))$[84]

Does FTB solve the problem?

FTB explains why S has now reason to prefer knowledge by citing other true beliefs S will

---

[81] "P[C|(D&~E)]< P[C|E] where C is the condition that you believe p tomorrow, D that you believe p truly today, and E that you know p today." Williamson 2000, p. 79.
[82] Presumably, Williamson is assuming that propositions have their truth values eternally, so that present truth entails future truth.
[83] Or to explaining successful action; Williamson is focusing on explaining action, regardless of its success.
[84] reading "sTBp" as abbreviating "s has a true belief that p", "K" as abbreviating "knows", and s ranging over cognizers, p over propositions.

likely have. And it's those true beliefs, in the case of each individual action, which explain the difference in successful actions. That is, in each token case, it looks like *beliefs* which cause the actions; whether or not they are knowledge is superfluous. And that makes it look like what's *really* responsible for differences in which actions are performed, not just in each token case but in general, is a difference in *beliefs* between S and S' (in cases where the relevant[85] motivational and background cognitive set is shared). And while the truth of the belief is relevant to explaining the *success* of the actions which are performed, at both type and token levels, the epistemic accretion on top of the true belief looks otiose.[86] So it isn't the epistemic status of knowledge which is really the difference-maker to actions. That, I take it, is the deep worry, which has so far eluded capture.[87]

We might try to capture this deeper worry by simply packing into the antecedent of the practical equivalence claim something about the true beliefs which will matter down the road.[88] But such a practical equivalence claim would be open to the same objection that afflicted PE2 and PE4 above. Suppose it were true. Clearly that would be relevant to the people it compares – i.e. those S and S' of whom the antecedent is true. S' would have no practical reason to prefer to be a knower like S. But precisely because people in that position are so different from most cognizers, this won't threaten explanations of MPE in terms of future true belief, FTB.

Taking such a practical equivalence claim to threaten the explanation of MPE in terms of FTB would be like taking the very small percentage of cases where HIV does not lead to AIDS to show that the effects of AIDS do not explain why, in general, there is reason to desire not contracting HIV. In fact, to take this version of practical equivalence to be problematic would be worse. After all, genetic testing might allow us to know precisely which actual individuals will fail to develop AIDS even if they get HIV, so that the general truth that HIV leads to AIDS might be *known* not to be applicable in a particular case. On the other hand, there are no actual people in the position of S and S', and so *a fortiori* none are known to be in that position.

So the tension between formulations of the practical equivalence claim which are too strong

---

[85] That is, whatever cognitive and motivational set *actually* happens to be relevant, in that particular case. Just to be clear: the problem in formulating the practical equivalence claim is coming up with a *general* account of what cognitive states are relevant. By pointing out that problem, I'm not denying that in particular cases, some cognitive states are causally salient to actions, and others are not.

[86] There are ways to resist this worry. One might just deny that there's any connection between type and token level explanation, here. There are certainly some reasons to doubt that one can always move from a single token level causal claim to the corresponding type level generalization, or from a type level causal claim to a token level causal claim which instantiates the type level claim (see, e.g., Hitchcock 1995). But this move is different: it's from a uniformity of token level explanatory claims to a type level generalization. It seems likely to me that there are intuitive counterexamples to the validity of that kind of inference, too; but it's enough for my worry here that the inference is *plausible*, even if deductively invalid, since all I'm trying to do is diagnose what remains troubling. Moreover, even if not deductively valid, this particular inference does seem to me to be a good one. It's the beliefs that are difference makers.

[87] In fact, as will become clear, I don't think that there's just *one* deeper worry, here, but many.

[88] In order to do this, we would construct true practical equivalence claims in the following way: for each bit of knowledge that p which S has, generate a set of mere true beliefs, P, by isolating the true beliefs which will later be responsible for some successful actions. Add to P the set T of true beliefs which S has because of her knowledge that p, but which don't cause successful actions, and so don't appear in P. Assign to S', in the antecedent of the equivalence claim, all the mere true beliefs in P ∪ T. If the consequent then compares cases where S and S' differ only with respect to the status (as knowledge or not) of the beliefs in P ∪ T, these will by construction of P be cases where S will φ iff S' will φ. By construction of P ∪ T, S and S' will also have the same true beliefs becaue of their cognitive states (though it's not true that they will in general have the same beliefs, since they may have very different experiences, cognitively isolated beliefs, and so on – this is one place where causal language would be important).

to be plausible, like PE1 and PE3, and formulations which are too weak to be really problematic, like PE2 and PE4, seems to generalize into a dilemma. Either a practical equivalence claim is implausible, or it's plausible but consistent with plausible explanations of MPE. I think this is strongly suggested by the reflections above, but I won't argue for it further. Rather, I'll suggest a different way to capture the deeper worry.

The structure of the problem revisited
This different way of capturing the worry understands the structure of the problem differently. Rather than having a distinct explanandum like MPE and searching for the problematic constraint on the explanation, we'll build the problematic practical equivalence claim into the explanandum.

To see both how to do this and why, think again about Socrates' reformulation of the practical equivalence claim: "Won't the one who always has correct opinion always hit the mark, so long as he opines correctly?" Socrates is not, on the face of it, comparing two cognitive states like knowledge that p and true belief that p, but two individual cognizers. And those two cognizers will differ only with respect to the epistemic status of their beliefs, and thus will be a kind of minimal pair for testing the hypothesis that the epistemic status of true beliefs is itself a difference-maker for successful actions.

To build this comparison into the explanandum, we need to ask not whether agents have reason to prefer knowing p to merely truly believing p, but rather whether agents have reason to prefer being in the total cognitive state of a knower to being in a different total cognitive state. Now, obviously, this is going to generate different problems depending on how that different total cognitive state is characterized. But it seems clear how Socrates, at least, would do so, if his first "always" and its coordinate "so long as" are together taken to mean something like "whenever a person with knowledge will have a true belief." For any knowledge the knower S has, S' will have mere true beliefs; but S' will *also* have true beliefs in anything which S has (or will have) a true belief in as a result of knowing something. I will call this cognitive state persistent true belief.

Persistent true belief is only a matter of what an agent *actually* will believe; it places no constraints on what one is likely to believe, or whether subjunctive conditionals about what one would believe are true, and so satisfies no safety, security, adherence, or other reliability conditions on knowledge. So, importantly, persistent true belief is not simply equivalent to knowledge on any externalist accounts of knowledge.

The problem so understood, then, is to explain what I'll call the persistent belief explanandum:

(PBE) In general, agents have reason to prefer knowledge to persistent true belief.

FTB will not explain PBE, since Percy the persistent true believer that p will have a future true belief if Knut the knower will,[89] by construction of persistent true belief. Similarly, since Percy will have the same true beliefs in p's kin that Knut will, there will be no difference between them

---

[89] I use the generic characters of Percy the persistent true believer and Knut the knower here and in the rest of the chapter to avoid confusing talk about the *likelihood* that a persistent true believer will have a certain belief. Of course, since the definition of persistent true belief will result in different sets of true beliefs when applied to different knowers, we can talk about the likelihood that an arbitrarily chosen persistent true believer of p will have a true belief that p; but this does not entail that an arbitrarily chosen persistent true believer is likely to have true beliefs: those beliefs may all be insecure, unsafe, unreliable, and so on.

with respect to true beliefs in p's kin, which might explain the greater value of knowledge over persistent true belief.

Moreover, it really is puzzling why PBE should be true. It seems plausible that two cognitive states, if they are alike with respect to the true beliefs they cause, must also be alike with respect to the actions they cause. If so, knowledge and persistent true belief are equivalent with respect to the actions they cause. And since the beliefs which explain those actions are true, it seems that the actions will be equally successful.[90]

II.   Other solutions, other problems.

Although FTB is Williamson's official strategy for explaining why knowledge is more valuable than mere true belief, he also distinguishes a kind of stubbornness as an *irrational* insensitivity to counterevidence, presumably in contrast to a *rational* sensitivity to counterevidence.[91] Of course, FTB can explain why knowledge is preferable to stubborn true belief in Williamson's sense. But persistent true belief is just as sensitive to the truth as knowledge is, in the sense that Percy is just as likely to have a true belief as Knut. So, although Knut the knower is a better diamond-thief than Trudy the mere true believer, he seems to be no better a diamond-thief than Percy the persistent believer. For if Knut retains his belief that the diamond is in the bedroom, after hours of searching, then by definition of persistent belief, so will Percy.[92]

However, if we take seriously Williamson's distinction between *rational* and *irrational* sensitivities,[93] that paves the way for a compelling explanation of PBE, since persistent true belief does not involve a specifically *rational* sensitivity to truth. That is, none of Percy's alteration or retention of belief is required to come about for the right reasons.[94] On the other hand, at least some of Knut's changes and persistence in belief must come about for the right reasons. So if there is some reason for agents to prefer that change and retention of beliefs happen for the right reasons – that is, to prefer to be *rationally* sensitive – then that would explain PBE.

One such reason has been advanced before.[95] Being rationally sensitive to evidence matters for persuading others, in the sense of getting them to share our beliefs. For instance, if Percy fails to respond *rationally* to an objection to p, he will fail to persuade some who might be persuaded if he

---

90 The practical equivalence in this sense of knowledge and persistent true belief seems also to undermine the value of the putative safety, security, sensitivity, reliability, etc. Perhaps those properties are themselves valuable, but I do not know of anything satisfying attempt to show that the specifically *modal* character of those properties is valuable, as opposed to a state which is indistinguishable from them in the actual world.

91 "Although knowing is not invulnerable to destruction by later evidence, its nature is to be robust in that respect. Stubbornness in one's beliefs, an irrational insensitivity to counterevidence, is a different kind of robustness; it cannot replace knowing in all causal-explanatory contexts, for the simple reason that those who know p often lack a stubborn belief in p. The burglar's beliefs need not be stubborn." Williamson 2000, p. 63.

92 Though I developed this thought independently, Sosa also hints at this problem for FTB: Sosa 2010, p. 187, fn. 15

93 repeated later: "Present knowledge is less vulnerable than mere present true belief to *rational* undermining by future evidence, which is not to say that it is completely invulnerable to such undermining." Williamson 2000, p. 79, emphasis mine. Although Williamson's sensitivities here are to evidence rather than truth, I take the idea of a rational sensitivity to transfer neatly from the one to the other.

94 Although of course some of them may, and indeed many probably will, humans being what they are; the issue here is that an arbitrary persistent true believer is *less* likely to have their future true beliefs come about for the right reasons than their corresponding knower.

95 Jones 1997, and, though not so explicitly, Craig 1999.

could respond to the objection, although, like Knut, he himself would retain his true belief.[96] Of course, Knut might fail to be able to respond to the objection, despite his knowledge – it happens all the time. Likewise, Percy might get lucky with a gullible audience. The point is just that Knut is *more likely* to be able to respond to the objection in a persuasive way than Percy is. And there are plenty of similar kinds of situations, which make it look like the probability of persuading someone that p is higher conditional on knowing p than on merely persistently truly believing p.

Since an ability to persuade others is in general of value, this fact about persuasion is a promising explanation of PBE – of a reason for us to prefer knowledge to persistent true belief, in general. That is, using "sCs'" to abbreviate "s comes into contact with s'":

(PRS) $(s)(s')(p).(Pr(s'TBp \mid sKp \,\&\, sCs') > Pr(s'TBp \mid sPTBp \,\&\, sCs')$

PRS, for "persuasion," says that knowers are more likely than persistent true believers to transmit their true beliefs to those around them. It is essentially a social and synchronic version of FTB; instead of measuring the effects of knowledge across time, it measures the effects of knowledge across believers.

A second reason to prefer that change and persistence in belief happen for the right reasons, however, has been neglected. Being rationally sensitive to truth matters for *teaching:* a kind of activity from which about 4% of people in the developed world make their living. So teaching, presumably, is of value. And, again, Knut is more likely to be able to teach what he knows than Percy is to be able to teach the things Knut knows and Percy merely truly believes. But teaching differs from mere persuasion in this way, that though it often requires getting others to share our beliefs, it also places constraints on how that is done.

One such constraint is that those we persuade must also come to have justification for the beliefs we persuade them of.[97] This gives another explanation of PBE, distinct from but parallel to PRS: that knowers are more likely to transmit *justified* beliefs to those around them than persistent true believers. That is the "rational persuasion" explanation:

(RPRS) $(s)(s')(p).(Pr(s'JBp \mid sKp \,\&\, sCs') > Pr(s'JBp \mid sPTBp \,\&\, sCs'))$[98]

There seem to me to be other constraints on teaching, as well. For instance, it seems to me that teaching requires more than simply testifying that p and being an epistemic authority for your listeners. Teaching p requires producing some evidence for p which is connected to p more directly than your testimony is. But this is not the place for an investigation of teaching. So I will use RPRS as an example of one of the advantages of being able to teach, namely the advantage of being more

---

[96] Of course, persistent true belief that p is just as likely as knowledge to involve true beliefs in p's kin. And those beliefs will sometimes allow for the persistent true believer to respond to objections. The claim here is just that knowledge is *more* likely to come with those responses (e.g. from propositions other than p's kin, or in cases where the persistent true believer has the right belief in one of p's kin with which to respond, but fails to connect it to p).

[97] That isn't the *only* additional constraint on teaching. In *Knowledge is Teachable* I consider several other plausible constraints on teaching.

[98] This may look like citing justification in order to explain the value of knowledge, but it's not subject to the same worry raised above, that practical equivalence had an equal tendency to undermine justification. The crucial difference is that, whereas practical equivalence appeared to threaten the preferability of justified true belief just as much as it threatened the preferability of knowledge, practical equivalence is not at all a threat to understanding the preferability of giving *others* justified beliefs. Moreover, the truth of RPRS entails the falsity of practical equivalence in some senses.

likely to give your hearers justified beliefs.[99]

Both PRS and RPRS give us explanations that are especially satisfying as a response to the deep worry about practical equivalence: they show that the apparent practical equivalence of true belief is an illusion. Knowers are, in general, better persuaders, and better teachers. So not all actions are like getting to Larissa, where all that matters to the success of the action is the truth of your beliefs. In particular, for teaching, rational sensitivity to evidence also matters to success. So, although it seemed plausible that knowledge and persistent true belief, because they are alike in the true beliefs which come with them, must be alike with respect to the successful actions they cause, this turns out to be wrong. The truth of your beliefs is not all that matters to the success of actions. The epistemic status of beliefs also matters to the success of at least some kinds of actions.

Moreover, Socrates must realize this in the *Meno*, for he treats knowers as having the ability to teach, and actual statesmen as being unable to teach because they have only true beliefs, just after our passage: "That is the reason why they cannot make others be like themselves, because it is not knowledge which makes them what they are …Therefore, if it is not knowledge, the remaining alternative is right opinion."[100] To my knowledge, no commentator has taken Socrates' hint, here.[101]

One might well worry that it is, again, only some true beliefs which make knowers more likely to persuade others – for instance, true beliefs about what to say in response to objections. It seems plausible there must be *some* set of true beliefs sufficient to produce all the same responses to objections that a knower would.

A given persistent true believer will typically already have *some* of those beliefs. For they will have all the true beliefs that a knower of p would have on account of knowing p. Those will include true beliefs in p's kin, for instance. So, where the resources to respond to objections come from beliefs in p's kin, and the persistent believer recognizes that they do, a persistent true believer will be equally likely to be able to respond to the objection. But persistent believers will not be perfectly parallel to knowers in their ability to respond to objections, for two reasons. First, knowers are more likely to have some non-belief factors which help them respond to objections. Second, there are causes of beliefs which are independent of their token knowledge state, so that persistent true believers will not be perfectly parallel to knowers with respect to their beliefs, either. Both of these reasons bear some unpacking.

Responding to objections requires recognition of a link between p and a response to p – call the response q. One way to recognize a link between p and q is to have a belief, for instance, a belief that "q is a reason for p." But that is not the only way to recognize the link. One might have a disposition to respond to objections to p by asserting q, without having an antecedent belief that there is a link between p and q. It may even be the case that, in the absence of that particular

---

[99] The advantage of being able to transmit justified beliefs to others depends on what precisely justification comes to. On very stringent views of justification, perhaps the probabilities on both sides of the inequality in RPRS would be very low. On less demanding views, they may be high on both sides. But on all views which capture something we might plausibly mean by "justified beliefs," I think, the inequality will be true.

[100] 99b7-c1: "διὸ δὴ καὶ οὐχ οἷοί τε ἄλλους ποιεῖν τοιούτους οἷοι αὐτοί εἰσι, ἄτε οὐ δι' ἐπιστήμην ὄντες τοιοῦτοι… Οὐκοῦν εἰ μὴ ἐπιστήμη, εὐδοξίᾳ δὴ τὸ λοιπὸν γίγνεται·"

[101] Indeed, commentators almost uniformly also take Socrates' solution only solution in the Meno to be given by "stability," and take FTB to capture stability. In *The Stability of Knowledge* I argue that, contrary to appearances, Socrates does not mean FTB by stability. Even if that is wrong, it's not obvious that stability is Socrates' only solution to the problem.

objection to p, a knower of p would be likely to *deny* that q is a reason for p. In that case, we would not want to say that the knower of p has even a dispositional belief that q is a reason for p. So it looks like one can be in a better position to respond to objections to p, by citing q, without any beliefs that q is a reason for p. And knowers will be more often in this position than persistent believers. So fewer persistent true believers will recognize that they have the resources to respond to objections.

Second, persistent true believers have the same true beliefs that knowers have *because of* their knowledge. For any knowledge the knower has, the persistent true believer has any true beliefs which the knower has *as a result of* their knowledge. This leaves open the possibility that knowers have other belief states that persistent believers do not have. Though this is not helpful for my purposes here, it clearly leaves open the logical possibility that knowers typically have some *false* beliefs that persistent true believers do not. But it also leaves open the possibility that knowers typically have some true beliefs which are not caused by their token knowledge states. For instance, it seems plausible that knowers are typically more careful reasoners, or more skeptical. Careful reasons are more likely to have true beliefs about whether inferences are good inferences. If this is right, then knowers will be more likely to be able to respond to objections to p, when the objection trades on poor reasoning. Knowers are more likely to be able to respond to bad reasoning.

So PRS and RPRS get their bite precisely because persistent true belief will still differ from knowledge in systematic ways that matter for responding to objections. But this is not to deny that there is some set of true beliefs – beliefs about reasoning, for instance, and beliefs which constitute recognition of links between p and responses to objections to p – such that someone with those beliefs would respond to objections just as well as someone with knowledge. Take the set of true beliefs which are causally relevant to persuasion, or to rational persuasion, but which a persistent true believer would lack, and simply add it to the persistent true believer's belief set, in order to create another kind of cognitive state to more closely rival knowledge. Call this new rival "articulate persistent true belief." Articulate persistent true belief more closely approximates knowledge than persistent true belief does. So another problem will arise, namely to explain why agents have reason to prefer knowledge to this even-closer competitor cognitive state. Both PRS and RPRS will be as hopeless in explaining why we have reason to prefer knowledge to articulate persistent true belief as FTB was in explaining why we have reason to prefer knowledge to persistent true belief.

But my claim is not that FTB fails to solve *any* problem, while PRS and RPRS do solve the only problem. Rather, my claim is that FTB fails to solve a deeper problem which PRS and RPRS do solve: they explain PBE. What is special about PBE is that it brings into question the value of the epistemic status of knowledge, in a way that the original conception of the problem – explaining MPE – does not.

Shedding light on PBE is compatible with there being still other versions of the Meno problem – Meno problems, as we might call them – which PRS and RPRS don't solve. The closer to knowledge we make its competitors, the closer we get to the question: why prefer knowledge to a cognitive state which has *exactly* the same practical effects as knowledge? Is there something which is unique to knowledge, and which gives us reason to prefer knowledge to *any* possible competitors?

Now we are running into a limitation of layman's questions about value. For if we make the competitor cognitive state close enough to knowledge, then it looks like they will be indistinguishable in general – in the sense of "in general" discussed earlier. And there will of course be nothing that makes knowledge preferable to an indistinguishable competitor. So there may simply be no answer to the layman's question about sufficiently close competitors.

On the other hand, it may be that, given sufficiently close competitors, the standards change, so that a layman's question collapses into a familiar philosophical question: is knowledge of final value? In Chapter 1, I argued for a skeptical answer to this question. Knowledge is not of final value. We do not always have pro tanto reason to prefer knowledge to mere true belief. If I am right, answering that question about final value is not the only Meno problem. It is one of many.

Nonetheless, there is something less than fully satisfying about citing anything which isn't absolutely specific to knowledge in our explanations of the versions of the Meno problem I've considered: MPE and PBE. And, while PRS and RPRS may pick out features that are *more* specific to knowledge than FTB does, they are still far from specific to knowledge – they are shared by articulate persistent true belief, for instance.

There are two alternative explanations which one might extract from Williamson and Hawthorne, which aim to explain why we have reason to prefer knowledge to any close competitor. Unfortunately, neither of them is very compelling.

Williamson argues that knowledge, unlike persistent true belief, can count as evidence. So he might also argue that we value knowledge because we value evidence. This might be a good explanation of why justified stubborn belief is of more value than mere persistent true belief. And it might generalize to everything else that falls short of being knowledge, if those things also fell short of being evidence. This would be an interesting link to pursue as an explanation of PBE, if it were more plausible that only knowledge is evidence.[102]

Hawthorne's thought is roughly that if one throws out a lottery ticket without *knowing* that it will lose, then throwing it out would be irrational, so that in general "one ought only to use that which one knows as a premise in one's deliberations."[103] This is a claim, I take it, about practical rationality. And, if it's true, then it offers an interesting explanation of PBE: PBE would be true because knowledge, unlike persistent belief, matters for the practical rationality of one's actions, and doing things *rationally* is of value. One might well doubt that we really have reason to prefer to be practically rational.[104]

But suppose we do. The claim that it is *knowledge* rather than, say, rational belief which matters for the practical rationality of actions is at best contentious.[105] Even if it is difficult for someone to regard themselves as licensed to use a proposition which they don't know in practical reasoning, surely that fact is piggybacking on a more general fact that it's difficult for someone to regard themselves as licensed to *believe* a proposition which they don't know. And it seems quite important to practical rationality of action that when we evaluate someone else's action, we can rate their actions as rational even if they used a false belief in their practical reasoning – provided that the false belief was epistemically rational. So it's not clear on his line whether or why it's *knowledge*, rather than the epistemic rationality of our beliefs, that we would have reason to prefer.

Even if these worries for Williamson and Hawthorne's accounts could be answered, it seems to me clear that their accounts suffer a common flaw. For even if we often have reason to desire to be practically rational, or to have evidence for our beliefs, we do not always and necessarily have reason to desire either of these things.

So while these proposals by Williamson and Hawthorne might pick out something specific

---

102 For a recent strengthening of arguments that evidence is not factive, and so not limited to knowledge, see Fitelson 2010.
103 Hawthorne 2004, p. 30
104 see, e.g., Kolodny 2005
105 cf. the account in Foley 2001

to knowledge, they won't pick out something we have reason to desire which is specific to knowledge. Thus they would be no improvement on RPRS, with respect to explaining PBE. They may give us complementary explanations of why knowledge is in general preferable to true belief. But they do not give us better or more satisfying explanations of why knowledge is in general preferable to true belief.

Although RPRS is not specific to knowledge, Socrates is quite clear that an ability to teach *is* specific to episteme. At *Meno* 87b-c, Socrates claims that

(TK)   x is teachable (διδακτόν) iff x is episteme (ἐπιστήμη)[106]

In context, this claim must mean that someone has some bit of episteme iff they can teach it.[107] It's not entirely clear what that ability to teach comes to, for Socrates, but as a rough and only slightly tongue-in-cheek guide, I suggest it's the kind of ability which would qualify someone for academic employment.

Unfortunately, whatever an ability to teach comes to, Socrates' claim about episteme is implausibly strong as a claim about knowledge on our conception of it. But what does that show? I suggest that one thing it shows is that Socrates feels very keenly the force of the deeper problem – explaining why we have reason to prefer knowledge to persistent true belief – and feels a need to respond to the problem. That is as it should be for Socrates, given his commitment to the practical importance of knowledge. It may be that we do not share that commitment with him. But perhaps the lesson is not that Socrates makes two implausible and connected claims, one about the practical importance of knowledge, and one about the connection between knowing and teaching. Perhaps the lesson is instead that Socrates is not interested in knowledge, on our conception of it, but in something different: something *better*.

---

[106] T → K: "If [virtue] is anything other than knowledge ... can it be taught? Or is it clear to anyone that a man is taught nothing but knowledge?" (87b6-c3). And, immediately, K → T: "if virtue is some knowledge (ἐπιστήμη τις), it would be clear that it is teachable" (87c5-6). Restated at 87c8-9: "if [virtue is] of one sort, then it's teachable; if of another sort, it's not teachable."

[107] As I argue in *Knowledge is Teachable*.

Chapter 3: The swamping problem.

In the last chapter, I argued that our reasons for desiring knowledge extend beyond our desires to secure the truth for ourselves, so that a truth-monist answer to the Meno problem is incomplete. In this chapter, I consider the "swamping problem" for truth-monism about epistemic value. I argue that the swamping problem constrains but does not refute a truth-monist account of epistemic value.

Truth-monism about epistemic value says that truth is the only thing that occupies a certain central place in an understanding of epistemic value. There are lots of ways of making out *how* truth is supposed to be central, or what the special kind of value is, of course. The task of this chapter is to get clearer on which of these truth-monist views are substantive enough to be interesting philosophical positions, but are still plausible. Coming to grips with the swamping problem will help us in that task.

In Zagzebski's original formulation of the swamping problem,[108] the problem was specifically directed against reliabilism. Her contention was that a reliably produced true belief was of no more value than mere true belief. A later analogy with a cup of coffee is supposed to support this. A good cup of coffee is no better for having been produced by a reliable machine – or by any particular kind of machine. If that contention is right, then it would be a consequence of the truth of reliabilism that knowledge was of no more value than mere true belief. But surely knowledge is of more value than true belief. So reliabilism must be wrong.

More recently, she and others have argued that the problem is a general one for a view they call truth-monism about epistemic value.[109] The idea is that the coffee cup analogy applies more generally. It's not just that being reliably produced doesn't make good coffee any better. It's that coffee which smells and tastes a given way is not made better by *any* property which is directed at making better coffee. We are, after all, holding the quality of the cup of coffee fixed. And if it is already a good cup of coffee, it's not made better by, for instance, having been made from beans with fewer quakers, as beans which don't roast right are called. Likewise, if the argument above is good against reliabilism, it also seems good against any view which says that the epistemic status of a belief is a matter of properties which are in some sense aimed at truth. And that is a good first approximation of what truth-monism says.

The basic structure of the problem can be helpfully formulated as an inconsistent triad. The first claim is truth-monism, however it turns out to be formulated. The second is a claim that truth-monism entails a certain claim about value – the "swamping claim," here the consequent of (2). The third is that the swamping claim is false. So the three claims, using "x>y" to abbreviate the claim that x has greater epistemic value than y (etc.), in roughly Pritchard's formulation, are:[110]

(1)   truth-monism
(2+)   If truth-monism is correct, then $(x)(y).$(if x is true, then $x \geq y)$[111]
(3+) $\neg(x)(y).$(if x is true, then $x \geq y)$

---

108 In Zagzebski 1996, pp. 300 ff, especially p. 303. Also taken up by Kvanvig 2003, pp. 45 ff.
109 Zagzebski 2004, Pritchard 2010 & 2011.
110 This differs from the formulation in Pritchard 2010, p. 15, in order to be neutral on the content of truth-monism.
111 Where x and y range over beliefs.

This formulation is helpful because it makes clear two sources of a basic tension, and formulates precisely what the tension is. On the one hand, we epistemically evaluate equally true things differently. Knowledge and mere true belief are equally true, but to call something knowledge is to evaluate it both epistemically and positively, whereas calling something a mere true belief is not to evaluate it in that way. On the other hand, truth can seem to be what really matters, epistemically speaking. This is the vague thought that truth-monism develops. But these two claims seem to be in tension. And (2+) formulates precisely why they are in tension: because anything that plays the special role which truth is supposed to play is "swamping."

Perhaps the coffee cup analogy generalizes further. The swamping claim in (2+) says, in effect, that true belief is as epistemically good as it gets. But, of course, *bad* coffee won't be any worse for having been unreliably produced, or any better for having been reliably produced. And by the same token, a good cup of coffee unreliably produced will be better than a bad cup of coffee freakishly produced by a reliable machine. So it looks as if the analogy to a cup of coffee motivates not just (2+), but also motivates the claim that false belief is as epistemically bad as it gets, and that true beliefs are always epistemically better than false beliefs, i.e. (2-) and (2*).

(2-)   If truth-monism is true, then (x)(y).(if x is false, then x≤y)[112]
(2*)   If truth-monism is true, then (x)(y).(if x is true & y is false, then x>y)

And these conflict with analogues of (3+):

(3-)   ¬(x)(y).(if x is false, then x≤y)
(3*)   ¬(x)(y).(if x is true & y is false, then x>y)

I. The 3s.

Consider what (3+) says: there is *something* of greater epistemic value than *some* true thing.[113] This is an extremely weak claim. It is entailed (on nearly indisputable assumptions: e.g. that there are some justified beliefs) by all the following much stronger claims, although even these claims seem almost trivially true to me.

(K>TB)   (x)(y).(if x is a knowledge state & y is a mere true belief, then x > y)
(JTB>UTB) (x)(y).(if x is a justified true belief & y is an unjustified true belief, then x > y)

Similarly, (3-) is entailed by the following claim which also seems trivially true:
(JFB>UFB) (x)(y).(if x is a justified false belief & y is an unjustified false belief, then x > y)

And (3*) is entailed by the almost as trivial:

(JFB>UTB) (x)(y).(if x is a justified false belief & y is an unjustified true belief, then x > y)

Why do these seem almost trivially true? Recall that ">" is an *epistemic* value relation.

---

112 Though I came to this thought independently, Carter and Jarvis forthcoming also suggest that the same reasoning which establishing the swamping claim in (2+) establishes the one in (2-); see their S4*, typescript p. 5
113 N.b.: the 3s are not simply comparing the epistemic value of some knowledge that p with a belief that p; they make the even more modest claim that there is *some* false belief which is epistemically better than some true belief.

40

Insofar as anyone has any handle at all on which evaluations are epistemic, justification is a specifically epistemic good, so that (JTB>UTB) and (JFB>UFB) seem trivially true. Knowledge is equally obviously an epistemic good, so that (K>TB) seems trivially true. And note that these generalizations need not be exceptionless or even true in general – provided that ceteris are sometimes paribus, they may be true only when qualified with "ceteris paribus." Still, they would entail the 3s. Nonetheless, no matter how obvious these claims seem, there is a gap between obvious and undeniable, and the literature contains one explicit objection to the 3s, one objection which can be extracted from Alston 2005, and another which suggests itself. I consider these in turn, below.

Note that the 3s entail nothing about what we have reason to care about, desire, or value. They don't entail the falsity of the claim that our reason to desire justified beliefs depends entirely on our reason to desire the truth.[114] Nor do they entail that we care more about knowledge than about mere true belief, any more than the claim that queening one's pawn without being checkmated being better *as a chess move* than moving into checkmate entails that all humans desire to queen their pawns without being checkmated more than they desire to move into checkmate. Perhaps someone simply wants to be done with the game, so they choose a bad chess move. Perhaps they don't really understand the rules of chess. But none of this matters for claims about which move is better as a chess move. In the same way, facts about what humans do or don't desire or value don't entail the truth or falsity of these claims about epistemic value.[115] And the 3s are about epistemic value.

Objection: the 3s are plausible only because of a double-desire illusion

Marian David's motivation for denying the 3s is roughly that he thinks we desire justification for the sake of truth, rather than the other way around. So it is possible that, if he were to distinguish questions about epistemic value from questions about what we have reason to desire, he would rescind his objection. Nonetheless, his objection bears consideration. He claims that our intuitions that the 3s are true

> "arise due to a confusion of sorts. They do not reflect any bonus of intrinsic value accruing to knowledge over and above (non-accidentally) true belief, nor do they reflect any intrinsic value accruing to justified belief that would be independent from the value of (non-accidentally) true belief; rather, they reflect our desire to have our desires satisfied."[116]

The idea here is that we have two desires – one for true beliefs, and another for justified beliefs. We form the second desire *only because* we have the first desire and believe that the best way to satisfy it is to have justified beliefs. But "it is nevertheless a real desire, just as real as the desire for true belief – desires for derived goods are no less real *as desires* than desires for basic goods."[117,118] And the satisfaction of more desires leads us to think that, e.g. justified true belief is epistemically better than unjustified true belief. So even though (K>TB), (JTB>UTB), and (JFB>UFB) are strictly speaking false, they *seem* true because in each case having x satisfies more desires than having y.[119]

---

114 In any event, as I argued in Chapter 2, this claim is false.
115 I argue for this claim in Chapter 1, sections III-IV.
116 David 2005, p. 310.
117 David 2005, p. 310.
118 This objection is echoed in Sosa 2010, p. 188, though with a twist that renders it not topical here.
119 As David admits, this won't work for (JFB>UTB), since in that case precisely one desire is satisfied on each side. About this case, he says, "intuition hesitates" (David 2005, p. 309). But it seems clear to me that intuition doesn't hesitate, especially once one is clear that the claim is about epistemic value. Second, it seems clear that if intuitions

But even if, in general, we make mistakes about relative value when more of our desires are satisfied, that won't explain why *these* claims are so intuitive, since in this case we could presumably become aware by reflection that the extra desire satisfied on the left hand side of each claim is a desire we have *only because of* our desire which is attained on both sides. And once we become aware of that, the confusion David proposes would surely dissolve, and we would come to realize that all these claims are false. But the claims are no less plausible after reading David and engaging in honest reflection: they still seem almost trivially true. So this challenge to the 3s fails; and I'm not aware of any other explicit objection to them in the literature.[120]

The objection from demarcation

Although Alston does not explicitly attack the 3s, he gives voice to a potential objection to them. The objection would be that we have to count truth as an epistemic value which makes the 3s false, in order to demarcate the class of epistemic evaluations – that is, in order to distinguish the epistemic evaluations from non epistemic evaluations.

> "in order to mark out the distinctively *epistemic* values of beliefs I have been led to do this [i.e. mark them out] by reference to the epistemic point of view, which I got at in turn from a consideration of the basic aims of cognition. And I do not see any equally effective way of distinguishing epistemic values of beliefs from others."[121]

Now, one might worry that Alston's way of demarcating epistemic evaluations is not very effective, either. But put that worry aside. For in Chapter I, I demarcated the class of epistemic evaluations in a very different way, by first taking paradigm cases of epistemic and non-epistemic evaluations, and then considering some that were less clear. The paradigm cases of positive epistemic evaluations were cases of justified belief – that's why I take the 3s to be obviously true.

But Alston might well disagree. He argues that "the widespread supposition that 'justified' picks out an objective feature of belief that is of central epistemic importance is a misguided one."[122] And so he might argue that what I cited as paradigm cases are not cases of epistemic evaluation at all, because they do not ascribe any determinate epistemic standing.

Alston might instead say that, while we can rely on these paradigm cases, they do not give us an equally *clear* or *precise* way to distinguish epistemic values of beliefs from others. And that is, I think, right: there is no equally clear and precise alternative. But part of the point of this chapter and the next two is to show what we lose when we prefer an account of epistemic value with more precise borders to an account of epistemic value which better captures our evaluative practice.

In this context in particular – that is, if Alston wanted to respond to the swamping problem by rejecting any of the 3s – preferring an account with precise borders would be throwing the baby out with the bathwater. For his account with precise borders counts being true as itself of epistemic value. But there seem to be *no* epistemic evaluations which are made true by the thing evaluated

---

did hesitate because UTB satisfies one desire and JFB satisfies another one, and if the desire satisfied by JFB were derived from the desire satisfied by UTB, then it would surely become clear on further reflection that, in fact UTB>JFB. And even if it weren't obvious that (JFB>UTB), surely it's also not clear after due reflection that UTB>JFB.

120 I suppose one might worry that "justification" is not always reflective of epistemic value, because of pragmatic encroachment. In that case one could simply substitute for "justification" in these four claims whatever turns out to be the epistemic core of justification.

121 Alston 2005, p. 33.

122 Alston 2005, p. 11.

simply being true.¹²³ If I say "your belief is true," that does not sound to me like a specifically epistemic evaluation. If I say "that was a lucky guess," that may be because your belief was true. But insofar as that is an *epistemic* evaluation, it sounds like a *negative* epistemic evaluation: your guess was lucky, so it didn't count as knowledge.¹²⁴

Finally, since denying the 3s involves denying existentials, it involves denying even our demarcational intuition about the Pascal's Wager case, at least about counterfactuals. If someone believed that god existed because of the practical benefits of doing so, their belief would be unjustified. But if it happened to be true, this Alstonian line would say that the belief was epistemically better than the most well-supported of false beliefs. So, in fact, this Alstonian response to the swamping problem seems to me worse than throwing the baby out with the bathwater. It completely undermines the handle I do have on what "epistemic" contributes to "epistemic evaluation."¹²⁵

Undermining explanation: Justification is about expected *epistemic value.*

Another strategy, not yet found in the literature so far as I know, would be to undermine the 3s by arguing that intuitions which seem to support them actually support claims not about epistemic value, but about *expected* epistemic value. Expected epistemic value would be what is relevant to rational belief, in roughly the way that expected value is relevant to rational action, and for roughly the same reason – a kind of lack of access to the truth. If so, the thought would be, then rational beliefs are of greater *expected* epistemic value than irrational beliefs. We think that they are actually of greater epistemic value, which is why we believe the 3s: but we're wrong, and only think that because we confuse expected epistemic value with epistemic value.¹²⁶

This objection doesn't give us reason to reject the 3s. First of all, this objection, like the demarcational objection above, assumes that truth is itself of epistemic value. And that seems implausible, as I pointed out in response to the demarcational objection. But consider, besides, that we're able to calculate the expected value of a choice only when we know the values of the possible payoffs. And this new objection simply assumes without argument that the values of the possible epistemic payoffs are as truth-monism together with the 2s would entail. It has to do so, if expected epistemic values are going to explain why we believe (K>TB) and the other principles like it. So this objection also begs the question against the 3s.

So the 3s still seem almost trivially true. And, if we've got to keep the 3s, then we have a constraint on truth-monism. Versions of truth-monism which make the corresponding 2s true, and so are incompatible with the 3s, must be rejected. The hard question is whether there are any versions of truth-monism which are plausible enough to have more than fringe appeal, but which are eliminated by this constraint, because they make the 2s true. In the next section, I'll begin looking into this question by considering the motivation for truth-monism, asking along the way

---

123 Thanks are due to John MacFarlane for pressing this worry.
124 This might sound like an independent argument against truth-monism: but truth-monism need not say that *being true* is itself of specifically epistemic value, as is clear on the official formulation of truth-monism, below.
125 Is this Alstonian line actually what Alston thinks? It sometimes seems to be, for instance when Alston 2005 argues that truth is an "epistemic desideratum" - i.e. a thing of epistemic value – on p. 40: "How could any property of a belief be better from [the epistemic] point of view?"
126 One picture which might inspire this response paints justification as parallel to excuses in ethics. If it turns out that you did something *morally* wrong, your lack of direct awareness of its wrongness might be an excuse. In the same way, if you had a false belief, you might be epistemically blameless if you were at least justified. But these cases are not clearly parallel.

how the view could be developed to avoid the 2s.

II. Truth-Monism.

Truth as the epistemic goal?

What special roles is truth often thought to play? One common thought is that truth is special because it functions as a goal of some kind.[127] So, for instance, Alston writes that "our basic cognitive goal, with respect to any proposition which is of interest or importance to us, is to believe it if and only if it is true."[128]

This role for truth does not by itself give rise to the swamping problem. For clearly one can think that that truth is the only epistemic *goal*, without thinking that truth "swamps" all other epistemic values, for at least two reasons. First, being a goal is not typically all that makes a difference to values in goal directed activities. It also typically matters *how* the goal is realized, and this is at the heart of the virtue-epistemological response to the swamping problem. Second, and more subtly, understanding a goal does not always give an understanding of all the phenomena directed at that goal.

The goal of a race may be to cross the finish line first, and the goal of a game may be to achieve a higher score, but there are typically better or worse ways of achieving those goals – more or less skillful, ethical, or beautiful ways. Some games are won by skillful playing, and others are won by intentionally fouling your opponent and not getting caught. Presumably, when we evaluate a game as "well played," we have the former kind of game in mind. In addition, there may be some value to having *achieved* a goal as the result of one's efforts, rather than the goal being realized through something other than your agency.[129] So, for instance, winning the game because of your playing might be better than winning it because the opposition defaulted or was disqualified. Hitting your target because of your skill in archery might be better than hitting your target because of an unanticipated gust of wind.

Both these kinds of value seem broadly independent of the particular character of the goal. So truth might well be the epistemic goal, but nevertheless justified beliefs might be a better way to reach that goal. Or justified beliefs might sometimes be the only way to reach that goal through your own agency. In either case, one could clearly hold that truth was the only epistemic aim, while maintaining and giving a plausible account of the 3s.[130]

More generally, not all goal-directed phenomena are explained by their relation to the goal. Why, for instance, do most sports games last less than a day? It's not the goal of the game that explains this, but facts about the players: that they need to eat and sleep, for instance. Or, to take a different kind of goal-directed activity, motion towards a goal may explain some contrastive explanations, without explaining all the possible contrastive explanations about the phenomena. For instance, if someone's goal is to get from San Francisco to Alaska, that may explain why they go north rather than south. But it may not explain why they take highway 101 rather than interstate 5, or vice versa. Or, again, for Aristotle, there will be some material causes even of animal

---

[127] For instance, this is the motivation Pritchard cites: "I think many are attracted to epistemic value T-monism, and attracted to it, at least in substantial part, because of the intuition that we started with: that belief in the relevant sense aims at truth (and all that this implies)" (Pritchard 2011, p. 246).
[128] Alston 2005, p. 32
[129] Greco 2009 is particular clear on this.
[130] This is not to say, for instance, that those accounts would be *true*. For criticism of this approach to the swamping problem, see especially Pritchard 2010, Chapter 2.

development, although the goal of animal development is a mature animal. These will be part of the goal-directed phenomena, but they will not all be explained by a relation to the goal. Some epistemic evaluations might also be like this. Perhaps religious beliefs, or beliefs about our own abilities, do not aim at the truth.[131] This too would render the view that truth is the aim of belief compatible with the 3s.[132]

Justification is for the sake of truth
Another common thought about the special role truth plays in epistemology is that justification is some sense simply instrumental for truth. Take, for instance, BonJour:

> "*if our standards of justification are appropriately chosen* [sic], bringing it about that our beliefs are epistemically justified will also tend to bring it about, in the perhaps even longer run and with the usual slippage and uncertainty which our finitude mandates, that they are true. If epistemic justification were not conducive to truth in this way, if finding epistemically justified beliefs did not substantially increase the likelihood of finding true ones, then epistemic justification would be irrelevant to our main cognitive goal and of dubious worth. It is only if we have some reason for thinking that epistemic justification constitutes a path to truth that we as cognitive beings have any motive for preferring epistemically justified beliefs to epistemically unjustified ones. Epistemic justification is therefore in the final analysis only an instrumental value, not an intrinsic one."[133]

Now, it seems to me that the charitable way to interpret BonJour here is as making a claim only about our reasons for desire or preference. He does, after all, explicitly put the point in terms of our "motive for preferring."[134] Perhaps his talk of *our* cognitive goal also favors this interpretation. And if this is BonJour's point, then he is not committed to claims about epistemic value. So he is not committed to denying the 3s, which are claims only about epistemic value. He is not describing the role truth and justification play in epistemology, but the role they play in our broader lives, even if he does not clearly distinguish between those two roles.

Truth is the only Intrinsic Epistemic Value?
Whether or not BonJour is committed to it, perhaps the claim that justification is only of instrumental epistemic value has some prima facie plausibility. So one might want to say that the special role truth plays in epistemology is the role of the only intrinsic epistemic value. But, again, the praxical value of justification could plausibly account for the 3s, even if truth were the only intrinsic epistemic value. Praxical value is a kind of value that something has not because of its intrinsic properties, but because of some facts about the causal genesis of the action and in particular the cognitive and motivational states of the agent, or in the epistemic case the believer. And these facts don't affect the individuation of the action or belief, and so don't matter to the intrinsic properties of the action or belief. For a moral analogue, suppose that Mary performs an action A for the right reason, and feels pleasure at it; this adds, on Aristotle's account, to the praxical value of the action. But that praxical value varies independently of the action itself, and so of its

---

131 In the locus classicus for the view that belief aims at truth, Williams is explicit that he's not going to talk about "religious and moral beliefs," although he contrasts those both to "straightforward factual belief" and to "belief as a psychological state." Even if belief "in the sense of a conviction of an ideological or practical character" (all p. 136, Williams 1973) is not of the same kind as straightforward factual belief, I take it, we might epistemically evaluate such states (see Chapter 1, section II). Even one such example would secure the 3s.
132 Though perhaps not with K>TB and the other claims like it above.
133 BonJour 1985, p. 8.
134 Though this phrase is certainly not the only thing relevant for interpreting BonJour 1985 on the subject of epistemic value, it is left out in quotes of the passage in both David 2001, p. 152, and Alston 2005, p. 12 & 30.

intrinsic value: Mary might have performed the same action for the wrong reason, or performed it for the right reason but felt no pleasure at it, in which case the same action, with the same intrinsic value, would lack the requisite praxical value. So, again, this claim about the role truth plays in epistemology is compatible with the 3s.

Truth is the only Final Epistemic Value?

A better way to capture the idea that justification is only instrumentally epistemically valuable would be by saying that truth is the only non-instrumental, or final, epistemic value. This is, for instance, how Pritchard formulates the target of the swamping problem.[135] And this claim has received significant scholarly attention.[136]

Many of the criticisms have focused on particular formulations of the claim that truth is the only thing of final epistemic value. For instance, it is clear that not just anything that raises the probability of true beliefs is of epistemic value. Many devices do that, but aren't of epistemic value. So the claim can't be simply that anything that makes us more likely to have true beliefs is of epistemic value. Nor can we simply restrict the principle to beliefs. A belief that one will survive an illness may raise the probability of survival, and so raise the probability that one will have true beliefs in any number of propositions. But any of these beliefs, including the belief that one will survive, will still be epistemically bad if it is not supported by one's evidence.[137] Cases like this show that the truth-monist view must be developed in a way that does not allow the wrong kind of trade-offs between the truth of one belief and the truth of others – a view that respects the "separateness of propositions," in Selim Berker's phrase.[138]

It is a curious fact about the literature on the topic that there is a dearth of defenders of truth-monist views against these objections. And without further development and defense, it is not clear whether there is any plausible truth-monist theory which says that truth is in some sense the only thing of final epistemic value. But suppose some such view were plausible as an account of epistemic value. Would it entail the swamping claims? That is, would it make the 2s true?

It seems to me that it need not. The swamping claims would not follow simply from claims that truth is the only thing of final epsitemic value. To see why, consider first a naive formulation of moral hedonism: pleasure is the fundamental moral value. Does this entail the moral analogue of the swamping claims, i.e. that any pleasant thing is morally better than any unpleasant thing? Surely not: it entails at most that that is true of certain things. For instance, the sort of hedonism Socrates attributes to the many in the *Protagoras* might entail that any *life* which is more pleasant is morally better, but since some pleasant *actions* lead to less pleasant lives, they turn out to be morally worse than unpleasant actions which lead to more pleasant lives. That sort of hedonism is a hedonism about lives, not actions.

Similarly, one might think that truth is the fundamental value in some more holistic way, for instance in the sense that believing a true *theory* is the only intrinsic epistemic value. In that case, justified beliefs would be epistemically good if they were in the right way instrumental for coming to

---

135 Pritchard 2010, p. 14.
136 Good critical starting points: Firth 1981 (with Chisholm 1991) and Kelly 2003. As far as I can tell, Chisholm was the only real defender of the view commonly criticized in the literature, though that may be as much as matter of other authors' relative lack of clarity in expressing their position (as in BonJour's case above).
137 Roughly this example comes up in Firth 1981.
138 Berker (unpublished), following Rawls criticism that classical utilitarianism does not "respect the separateness of persons."

have true theories.¹³⁹ So individual unjustified true beliefs might well turn out to be worse than individual justified false beliefs. So this kind of truth-monist view is consistent with the 3s. That is not to say, of course, that it is clear how the view would go, or that it has a good account of why the 3s are true. It is not. The point is just that this kind of holistic view, on which justification is instrumental for truth, need not fall prey to the swamping problem.¹⁴⁰

Another reason this sort of view might escape the swamping problem is that there is more than one way to be instrumentally valuable, and the 2s only holds for some of those ways. So, depending on the "for the sake of" relation, some things may be valuable only for the sake of other things, but still be independently valuable. For instance, on one interpretation of Aristotle's account of happiness in *EN*,¹⁴¹ the constituents of happiness such as character-virtue are in some sense instrumentally valuable for the sake of happiness. But this doesn't show that two happy lives are equally good, since one may include some constituents of happiness which the other lacks entirely, or may simply include more of one. In the same way, some ways of having true beliefs might be better than others, and some ways of having false beliefs might be better than others. It is harder to see how this strategy could account for (JFB>UTB), and so for 3*, but perhaps that difficulty is not insuperable.

Finally, it's not clear why a view on which truth is the only final epistemic value should deny 3-. Even if truth were the only non-instrumental epistemic value, we could still distinguish between the value of different false beliefs, for instance in terms of how likely they are to be true. So, insofar as the coffee analogy is a good guide to the problem, it looks like the swamping problem is not a problem for view that truth is the sole final epistemic value.

These reflections suggest is that the swamping problem is not a problem for all the members of the family of views on which truth is the only thing of final epistemic value. But it is another question whether any of those theories would give a plausible account of epistemic value. In particular, if they count being true as an epistemic good, that is a mark against them, since being true does not seem to be a specifically epistemic good. And, of course, they would have to respect the "separateness of propositions." It is not clear that such a theory is available, and so it is not clear whether the swamping problem does rule out all the plausible members of the family of views on which truth is the only thing of final epistemic value.

Relations to truth are the sole fundamental explainers of epistemic value

But if the swamping problem is not a problem for all versions of the claim that only truth is of final epistemic value, why think that the swamping problem threatens only versions of that claim? The motivation for truth-monism does not seem to dictate that truth must play the role of sole final epistemic value. And by lifting that restriction, we might cast a wider net, and so identify a more interesting philosophical position.

Indeed, although Pritchard's official account of truth-monism is in terms of final epistemic value, he explains that view by saying that though truth-monists allow that other things may be epistemic goods, they hold that some relation to true belief is "what makes these goods epistemic

---

139 This is one way of making out the position in Alston 1985 quoted as an expression of truth-monism in David 2001, p. 151, where Alston talks about minimizing false beliefs and maximizing true beliefs "in a large body of beliefs."
140 Perhaps an explanationist view of epistemic value, like Lycan 1985, on which epistemic value is a matter roughly of having better explanations, could provide the holism to be combined with the claim that justification is instrumental for truth.
141 The locus classicus of this interpretation is Ackrill 2001.

goods."[142] So, to cast our wider net, we might instead take truth-monism to say that the special role truth plays in epistemology is that it is the fundamental explainer of epistemic evaluations.

This formulation seems to capture the crucial intuition in the coffee analogy. The fundamental explainer of the goodness of coffee is its some combination of perceptible properties, like its flavor, smell, and mouth-feel. The production of the coffee may alter the chances of the coffee counting as good, but it does not at all contribute to the explanation of why the coffee counts as good. Thus, insofar as the coffee analogy is a guide to the swamping problem, the swamping problem seems to afflict some members of a wider family of views which say that truth is the only fundamental explainer of epistemic value. A rough formulation of that family of views takes them to have the form TM:

(TM) For all true epistemic evaluations E, where E attributes V to x, there is a set of relations {R} which (i) x bears to the truth of x (and to nothing else) & which (ii) explain why x counts as having V

Before moving on, some clarifications of the content of TM are in order. First and foremost: relations come cheap. There will be many relations which fit clause (i) of TM. But very few of them will come anywhere close to satisfying clause (ii). For most relations between a belief and its truth will cross-cut epistemic value. For instance, the relation which holds precisely when the belief is true will cross-cut epistemic value, since some false beliefs are epistemically better than some true beliefs. Such relations have no chance of explaining epistemic evaluations.[143]

The idea behind the parenthetical restriction in (i) is that *only* truth plays the role of fundamental explainer. So it rules out, for instance, the relation that holds precisely when an ideal reasoner would have the belief. That is not a relation to the truth of the belief alone. In an intuitive sense, it is also a relation to the ideal reasoner.[144] Similarly, the relation that holds precisely when x amounts to knowledge will not count as a relation to the truth of the belief alone.[145]

This formulation also has the considerable advantage that it is attributable to a broader swathe of philosophers, on charitable interpretations, than the earlier formulations of truth-

---

142 Pritchard 2011, p. 246.
143 This may sound surprising, in context. Isn't this just what the swamping problem says that truth-monists are committed to – i.e. denying the 3s? Yes – but the problem is supposed to be that truth-monists are committed to this unfortunate consequence by their theory, not simply that this *is* their theory.
144 This qualification is not intended to bear too much weight, but to be a placeholder for a restriction which is motivated by the idea that truth monist theories say that truth is the *only* thing that plays the role of fundamental explainer of epistemic value. If the relations are relations the belief bears to truth *and* to something else, it no longer looks like truth is the only thing that plays that role. The account of epistemic value I propose in Chapter 5 is like this: the relations that matter are not just relations to the truth of the belief in question, but are also relations to other cognizers. So that account is not a truth-monist theory. TM roughly captures this intuition, but to make it really precise would of course require significant development.
145 In this case, one might wonder why "x is formed by a process which reliably produces true beliefs" does not count as a relation to more than just the truth of the belief. After all, it mentions a process, and doesn't explicitly mention the truth of x. I do not have a theory of how to understand relations which makes clear why reliable production does not introduce an extra relatum, while the relation that holds when x amounts to knowledge does mention another relatum, viz. knowledge. And perhaps no theory could be given. If so, that would be a problem for formulating truth-monism. But since my goal here is to criticize truth-monism, I will leave it to truth-monists to bear out the intuition, which I share, that there is some difference between these relations: that it is really only *truth* that does the explaining, in the case of a reliable process, while it is not only truth which does the explaining, but also knowledge, in the other case. Thanks are due to John MacFarlane for pressing this worry.

monism. In the next section I'll review some of these philosophers, before moving on to consider which versions of TM make the 2s true.

Truth-monists

It can be difficult to tell whether a philosopher believes TM. For instance, Alston 2005 gives one of the more explicit discussions available of which evaluations are epistemic and why. But the casual reader might conclude that Alston is *not* a truth-monist. For, after claiming that truth is the most "basic" and "central" thing of epistemic value[146], he adds "the crucial point is that the most *basic* aim of cognition is not the only thing aimed at by cognition, not even the only thing aimed at from the standpoint of that most basic aim." So he appears only to be making a claim about "the most basic aim." But then he immediately continues: "That is because other features of belief are also desirable from the standpoint of that basic aim *because they are related in various ways to it*."[147] And this seems to say that the any other aim of cognition is of epistemic value because it is related to the basic aim of cognition, i.e., truth. That's as clear a statement of truth-monism as any available.

But Alston's commitment to truth-monism is made clear by another test which also happens to widen the net considerably. In later discussion, he rejects other candidate desiderata, such as Foley rationality,[148] as not properly *epistemic* desiderata because they lack the proper relation to truth. This inference, from lack of a proper relation to truth, to lack of epistemic value, would not be valid unless TM were right: so Alston is also committed to truth-monism by this inference. And other philosophers make similar inferences.

One of Williams James' arguments in *The Will to Believe* certainly seems to. James assumes that it is always epistemically permissible to believe p when the probability[149] of p being true is at least ½. This would not be necessarily true, if there might be something other than this way of being related to truth which accounted for some epistemic permissions or lacks of permission. So James is assuming that this probabilistic relation to truth is the only difference-maker to this kind of epistemic evaluation. He might, of course, invoke other difference-makers in explaining other evaluations. But then why should epistemic permissions be different? Since the drift of James' argument is that what matters, epistemically speaking, are the chances of gaining the truth and being in error, it seems likely that James is simply assuming that these are the only difference-makers to any epistemic evaluations.

In Graham Priest's argument against the standard objections to the rationality of believing a contradiction, he responds to one objection in a way that may seem to commit him to something like truth-monism. The objection is that, if there is sufficient evidence that p is false, one ought [epistemically] rationally to reject it. Priest responds: "Truth is, by its nature, the aim of cognitive processes such as belief... Falsity, by contrast, is merely truth of negation. It has no independent epistemological force. One should not, therefore, reject something simply because its negation turns out to be true."[150] But why think that falsity, even if that is distinct from untruth, lacks independent epistemological force? Presumably because Priest assumes something like truth-monism.[151]

In Roger White's argument against epistemic permissivism, he argues that forming a certain belief under certain conditions would be epistemically equivalent to taking a belief-inducing pill with

---

146 I take it that Alston's "epistemic desideratum" is roughly synonymous with my "thing of epistemic value."
147 Alston 2005, p. 36.
148 Alston 2005, p. 45ff.
149 In some sense: but any sense will work, here, I think.
150 Priest 1998, p. 421.
151 Or something like it: for my purposes, it's still a recognizably truth-monist view if it cites relations to untruth.

49

a 50% chance of giving one a true belief: "is there any advantage, from the point of view of pursuing the truth, in carefully weighing the evidence to draw a conclusion, rather than just taking a belief-inducing pill? Surely I have no better chance of forming a true belief either way."[152] But parity with respect to the chance of gaining the truth is only decisive for epistemic evaluation if truth-monism is true – in fact, only if a pretty implausible version of truth-monism is true.

Alston, James, Priest, and White form a fairly diverse group. So a fairly broad spectrum of actual philosophers seem to be committed to TM. And perhaps some virtue epistemologists are caught in the net, too. If praxical epistemic value is a matter of having achieved true beliefs through one's own agency, then it will be a matter of the belief standing in a relation to truth: having achieved it. This will be a different relation to truth from, for instance, a belief being reliably produced, or safe, or sensitive to the truth. So the virtue epistemologist may cite different relations to the truth. But if a virtue epistemologist only cites relations to the truth, they will be truth-monists according to TM.

III. The 2s.

The 2s are not obviously true, on this conception of truth-monism. But neither are they obviously false. On the one hand, it's difficult to explain why *being* true should be the favored relation to truth. On the other hand, it's difficult to give a plausible truth-monist account against which the coffee analogy has no force. I do not know of any good explanation of why being true should be the favored relation to truth, but neither do any of the alternatives in the literature seem plausible.[153] So, in this section, I'll briefly describe the two alternatives in the literature, and why they are unsatisfying. Then I'll suggest an alternative account of epistemic value on which it doesn't matter whether the analogy has force, because it is not implausible to think that the fundamental explainers are swamping.

Consider a counterexample to an apparent analogue of the swamping claim. Investment is aimed at, and in some sense all about, profit. But it also takes into account the risk involved in an investment. That's why an account in an FDIC-insured bank with a 5% annual return is a better investment than an account at an uninsured bank with the same 5% annual rate of return.[154] It's a better investment because there are circumstances where the account at the uninsured bank becomes worthless, because the bank fails. Now, if the value of maximizing profit were swamping, and the uninsured bank did not fail, these accounts would be equally good investments. But it seems clear that they wouldn't be equally good investments. So the value of profit is not swamping for investment-goodness.

However, this does not show that there is no analogue of the swamping problem in the neighborhood. The analogue of the swamping problem[155] would ask, when both investments had paid out at year's end, whether the payout from the insured bank was better for having come from a less risky investment. And there the answer seems to be that it would not be.

---

152 White 2005, p. 448.
153 Pritchard 2010, p. 16: "I can see no way of objecting to [2+], nor am I aware of any good objections to this thesis in the literature." This claim postdates, in publication, Goldman & Olsson's 2009 conditional probability solution, which I consider below.
154 This example is a foggy remnant in my memory of one used by Rusty Jones in a talk at the West Coast Plato Workshop 2011.
155 I.e. of the 2+/3+ problem.

Note that these answers are not in tension. The less risky *investment* is better, but in this token case (as in many others) it will have an equivalent *payout*. It seems to me that there are two lessons to take from this example. First, that there are some evaluative domains where the fundamental explainer's presence does not swamp the value of other relations to the fundamental explainer, like goodness-as-an-investment. But, second, there are other evaluative domains where the fundamental explainer's presence does swamp the value of other relations to the fundamental explainer, like goodness-as-a-payout. After all, if the riskier investment had been much riskier, but had paid out very slightly more, it would have been a worse investment, but the payout would have been a better payout.

The problem with the two alternatives in the literature is that they identify plausible domains of epistemic evaluation where the value of truth is not swamping. But their story does not generalize, so it does not remove the force of the analogy in the original case, i.e. in the evaluations which entail the 3s. So they do not adequately respond to the problem.

The first proposal is made by Goldman and Olsson.[156] The essence of the proposal is that the property of being produced by a reliable process makes a belief more likely to persist.[157] This, they say, makes a situation where one has a reliably produced true belief epistemically better than a situation where one has a true belief not reliably produced.[158] But this is comparing states of affairs, not beliefs. It seems plausible that the state of affairs would be made better by this relational property. But it seems implausible that this makes the belief itself better. Compare: that a spouse has good relatives makes the state of affairs of having that spouse better. But does it make the spouse better? The added value in the state of affairs seems external to the spouse. And epistemic evaluations seem like evaluations of the spouse, in this way.[159] So Goldman & Olsson's proposal sounds like changing the subject: we wanted to know why the belief was better, and they instead explained why a state of affairs containing the belief was better.

Carter & Jarvis are sensitive to this concern, but try to explain why the belief itself is better for being justified:

> "... beliefs are ongoing *states*, not events with a past terminus. Just as the work of maintaining a clean house, the work of properly managing a belief is never over. One continues to have to manage the belief properly long after its acquisition; one might very well reflect on it today, and ultimately give it up tomorrow. 'Winning' for a belief is something ongoing rather than something that is, at some point, completed. Consequently, there is nothing obviously absurd about thinking that there continues to be instrumental e[pistemic] value even when the epistemic good is already present."[160]

---

156 Goldman & Olsson 2009, defended further in Olsson 2011, though I see no response to what seems to me the real worry.
157 The proposal basically turns FTB from Chapter 2 into a property of the belief in question.
158 Goldman & Olsson 2009, p. 28: "in both situations you believe truly that the road to Larissa is to the right (p) after receiving the information. On the simple reliabilist account of knowledge, you have knowledge that p in Situation 1 but not in Situation 2. This difference also makes Situation 1 a more valuable situation (state of affairs) than Situation 2. The reason is that the conditional probability of getting the correct information at the second crossroads in greater conditional on the navigation system being reliable than conditional on the navigation system being unreliable."
159 Another problem with this account is that it doesn't vindicate (K>TB) or the other claims like it as universal generalizations. But since (K>TB) is a claim about epistemic value, it seems to me to be exceptionless, in a way that MPE in Chapter 2 was not. This response to the swamping problem rests, I think, on the confusion between epistemic value and value simpliciter clarified in Chapter 1.
160 Carter and Jarvis forthcoming, typescript p. 11 (in section 4, *A Misguided Analogy*).

Now, perhaps this is right about beliefs. Perhaps we should evaluate a belief over a span of time, and justification will be instrumental in maintaining the true belief. But even so, we would need only to refine the 3s slightly to revive the problem. For now we will ask not about beliefs – those ongoing states – but about belief slices. Isn't it still obvious that a justified false belief-slice is *epistemically* better than an unjustified true belief-slice? A theory of epistemic value which was inconsistent with versions of the 3s about belief slices would be just as bad as a theory of epistemic value which was inconsistent with the 3s as stated.

In Carter and Jarvis' account of the swamping problem, this response to the force of the analogy does not occupy center stage. What does occupy center stage is an argument that the analogy proves too much. Not only does it support the 2s, it also supports analogues of the 2s for other monist positions about epistemic value. If one were a knowledge monist, for instance (substituting "knowledge" for truth in TM, above), then the force of the analogy would entail that any belief which failed to be knowledge was equally bad (the analogue of 2-). And that seems highly implausible, as they point out. This is a serious prima facie problem for knowledge-monism.[161]

But Carter and Jarvis are wrong to claim that the 2s appear "to be problematic whether or not one thinks that truth is the sole epistemic good. Consequently, the right response, we think, is to reject [the 2s]."[162] For there is a monist theory of epistemic value on which the swamping claims are plausibly *correct*. Suppose that instead of knowledge, we let the relation to truth which matters for truth monism be the evidential support relation. Then we would get the following analogues of the 3s:

(4+) $\neg(x)(y).$(if x is better supported by evidence than y, then x > y)
(4-) $\neg(x)(y).$(if x is worse supported by evidence than y, then x < y)

But the 4s are very plausibly false. They say that there is some belief which is better supported than another but epistemically worse, or worse supported and epistemically better. And those claims would be broadly contested.[163]

So the force of the coffee cup analogy, if it applies to this theory, does not show that there is a problem with the theory. The epistemic value of evidential support may well be swamping, but that is not clearly a problem for this theory. That is one mark in its favor. Another is that the theory is very plausible – more plausible than any of the other truth-monist theories considered so far, it seems to me.

IV.   Pulling the threads together.

The property of being true does not seem to be of epistemic value. And the fact that we often have reason to desire justification as a means to truth is irrelevant to a theory of epistemic value. So why put the property of *being true* at the center of a theory of epistemic value, even a

---

[161] I do not take this to be a *fatal* problem for knowledge-monism. But there is no well-developed knowledge-monist account in the literature, and it is very puzzling how knowledge could explain, for instance, the epistemic betterness of justified but Gettiered beliefs. Besides, a serious treatment of knowledge-monism would take more space than is available here.
[162] Carter & Jarvis forthcoming, typescript p. 10 (end of section 3).
[163] That is not to say that the 4s would be universally contested. One might think, for instance, that knowledge is always better than Gettiered true belief, even if the evidence better supports the Gettiered true belief. But my point here is just that, whereas the 3s seem clearly true, the 4s seem very plausibly false.

52

truth-monist theory? We can vindicate the idea that *truth* is at the center of a truth-monist theory by instead making truth the fundamental explainer of epistemic value, as TM says it is.

The most plausible truth-monist theory of epistemic value put forward so far is the theory above, against which the force of the coffee analogy is unproblematic. That theory says that epistemic value is a matter of evidential support. Better supported beliefs are epistemically better. This "evidential" theory is one of the theories which I will consider, and raise problems for, in Chapter 4. And this qualifies as a truth-monist theory, since evidence is evidence for the truth of beliefs. It just specifies that the relation to truth which matters is the evidential support relation.

Perhaps there are other truth-monist theories of epistemic value which similarly escape the swamping problem. For instance, perhaps a theory in terms of likelihood of truth could be made out. It would say that the more likely a belief is to be true, in some sense of likelihood (this is a major devil in the details), the epistemically better it is. I will certainly not *defend* this kind of theory of epistemic value. But, because that many others might be attracted to it, I will also consider this "likelihood of truth" theory in Chapter 4. In fact, it will turn out that in the problem cases, judgements of likelihood of truth and evidential support do not come apart – as, presumably, they rarely would, in any notion of likelihood of truth which could plausibly play the role of fundamental explainer in a theory of epistemic value.

This leaves two kinds of theory of epistemic value which have been much discussed in the literature, but which I will not explicitly consider in Chapter 4: virtue epistemological theories and reliabilist theories.

If the drift of this chapter has been right, then reliabilists should stick to their guns in responding to the swamping problem, but not in the way they have done. They should instead promulgate a straightforward theory of epistemic value on which the more reliably produced a belief is, the epistemically better it is.[164] If that theory of epistemic value is problematic, it will be because it does not adequately explain some epistemic evaluations – not because it is inconsistent with the 3s. I think it would get the epistemic facts on the ground wrong. In particular, a reliabilist theory would get the same cases wrong which, in Chapter 4, I raise as problems for the theories in terms of evidential support and likelihood of truth. But for the sake of simplicity, since reliabilism has relatively fewer defenders than the theories in terms of evidential support and likelihood of truth would, I will not explicitly consider reliabilist theories in Chapter 4.

If all this is right, then virtue epistemological theories do not receive special support from the swamping problem. Thus they, too, must be judged primarily on their accommodation of our intuitions about epistemic value, rather than on their ability to solve the swamping problem, or to explain the value of knowledge. And since, just as in the case of reliabilism, virtue epistemological theories of epistemic value have relatively fewer defenders than the theories in terms of evidential support and likelihood of truth, I won't explicitly consider them in Chapter 4, although I think the problems I raise would also be problems for virtue epistemological theories.

---

164 This is only intended to be a roughing-out of the theory. More complicated reliabilist theories, e.g. those which include a separate anti-Gettier clause, will of course give rise to more complicated theories of epistemic value.

Chapter 4: Two New Problems.

At the end of Chapter 3, two truth-monist theories of epistemic value seemed to be most promising. The evidential theory says roughly that evidence is the only epistemic concept we need in order to understand all true epistemic evaluations. The likelihood of truth theory, on the other hand, says that likelihood of truth, in some sense of 'likelihood,' plays that role instead. In this chapter I consider four challenges to these two theories. Since there do not seem to be any more plausible truth-monist theories of epistemic value, these challenges also constitute challenges to truth-monism.

Of these four challenges, the first two turn up only constraints on plausible ways of developing the theories. The third challenge, however, shows that the theories thus constrained get the lower margins of epistemic evaluation wrong. That is, they count as equally epistemically bad some pairs of beliefs which are maximally countersupported by one's evidence and maximally unlikely to be true, but are not equally epistemically bad. And the fourth challenge provides an argument independent of those constraints that these two apparently promising accounts of epistemic value also get the upper margins wrong.

Before turning to these challenges, it will be helpful to get clearer on the two promising theories of epistemic value from Chapter 4, and to consider a few initial dissatisfactions one might have with them.

The simplest version of the evidential theory says that a belief is epistemically valuable in proportion to its degree of support by the believer's total evidence. Better supported beliefs are epistemically better. Beliefs that are as maximally well supported – that is, supported as well as possible[165] – are as epistemically good as possible. Beliefs that are maximally countersupported – that is, as poorly supported as possible – are as epistemically bad as possible. And if anything other than a belief is epistemically good or bad, it is so because of some relation it has to epistemically good or bad beliefs. So, for instance, we might say that one cognizer is epistemically better than another if they tend to have epistemically better beliefs.

On this simple theory, all that matters to the epistemic value of a belief is a single relation to evidence: that it is supported by the evidence a believer has. But a canny evidential theorist will want to accommodate cases where a believer *has* total evidence which supports their belief, but does not *use* that evidence in forming the belief. So they will add a distinct relation to evidence, a basing relation, that will add epistemic value on top of merely *having* evidence which supports a belief.[166]

So the evidential theory is not restricted to a single relation to evidence. But note that, even on this revised evidential theory, if a belief is maximally well supported by the believer's total evidence, and the believer bases their belief on that evidence, the belief will be maximally epistemically good. So this revised theory still bears out the intuition that epistemic value is really all about the fit between beliefs and a believer's total evidence.

Is the evidential theory a truth-monist theory? That is, does it bear out the idea that

---

165 What I'm assuming here is that, for any token belief at a particular time, there is some determinate limit to the degree of evidential support. On a 0-n scale of evidential support, that may be n; or it may be less than n. That is, the limit of evidential support for a given token belief may be lower than the limit for any beliefs. For my purposes here, all that matters is that there is a determinate answer which holds for token beliefs at a time.

166 As do Feldman and Conee 1985, p. 93

epistemic value is all about relations to truth? The answer to this question depends chiefly on whether there is a way to understand the concept of evidential support along the lines of confirmation theory. That is, it depends on whether we can understand the evidential support of a belief as a matter of the degree to which some body of evidence confirms the belief, where "confirms" is a technical term that picks out some probabilistic relation between the evidence and the truth of the belief.[167] If evidential support can be understood in terms of a probabilistic relation to the truth of the belief, then an evidential theory of epistemic value is a truth-monist theory. If it cannot be understood in some such way, then an evidential theory is not a truth-monist theory.

If the evidential theory is not a truth-monist theory, then a truth-monist might prefer to take refuge in the best account of confirmation. Such an account might be thought of as an enlightening precisification, or rational reconstruction, of evidential support. For this reason, I think many philosophers who would be attracted to truth-monism in the first place might be tempted to spell out their theories of epistemic value without making use of the concept of evidential support, and would instead skip straight to confirmation, or likelihood of truth.[168]

I'll call this theory the "likelihood of truth" theory of epistemic value. Likelihood of truth for this theory is strictly parallel to evidential support in the evidential theory, where the meaning of "likelihood of truth" will be fixed by some favored measure of confirmation. So this theory says that beliefs which are more likely to be true, on the proper measure of confirmation, given the believer's total evidence, are epistemically better. Beliefs which are maximally likely to be true are maximally epistemically good.[169] And so on.

Perhaps there are other ways to spell out what "likelihood of truth" might mean, on which probabilistic relations to true belief are not given by any plausible measure of confirmation. But I think it will be plain that, in the problem cases I will consider, *any* plausible theory will say that the likelihood of truth is minimal, or maximal, as the case may be. So I will leave the likelihood of truth view to be further explained and defended by those who find it more appealing than I do.[170]

In the rest of the chapter, I'll be considering cases in which evidential support and likelihood of truth march together. So, for the sake of brevity, I'll sometimes speak just of evidential support. But all the points I will make could equally well be put in terms of likelihood of truth, I think, on this understanding of likelihood of truth.

Both the evidential and likelihood of truth theories seem plausible.[171] They give quite

---

167 For general discussion of this and other ways to understand evidence, see Kelly 2006; for a survey of different probabilistic measures of confirmation, see Fitelson 1999.
168 And other philosophers might simply find the view congenial. For instance, Fumerton 1995 formulates his "principle of inferential justification" (p. 36) in terms of the relation "E makes probable P," plus a recursion clause about being justified in believing E.
169 In order to be charitable, I'll also simply assume that truth-monists will either give an account of likelihood on which necessary truths and falsehoods (e.g. Goldbach's conjecture) may have non-extreme epistemic probabilities, or they will give an account of a relation to truth other than likelihood of truth, in order to handle the varying epistemic goodness of beliefs in propositions known to be necessary, and so known to be either maximally or minimally likely. Otherwise truth-monists would not be able to explain the epistemic differences between beliefs in propositions which are known to be necessary, and which happen to have the same truth value. Besides, there seems to me some theoretical motivation for treating evidence for necessary propositions separately.
170 There is to my knowledge no attempt to develop such a theory in the scholarly literature on epistemic value, though it would fit well with many epistemological views.
171 This is not to say unproblematic. Likelihood of truth theories, in particular, faces a serious problem in trying to give an account of lotteries. Those difficulties do not as obviously or as trenchantly afflict evidential theories. So it

plausible explanations of a wide range of epistemic evaluations. Beliefs which are supported by evidence, or are likely to be true, are epistemically better than beliefs which aren't. And beliefs which are *better* supported by evidence, or are likelier to be true, and epistemically better than beliefs which are worse supported, or less likely to be true. But these facts do not show that the two theories are correct. For they also make predictions about cases where beliefs are equally supported by the evidence, or are equally likely to be true.

The simple version of the evidential theory, for instance, says that all such beliefs are equally epistemically good. More complicated theories will require more complicated equivalence claims, for instance that two beliefs are both based on evidence which supports them equally well. But the point is that these theories will say, of some such beliefs, that they are equally epistemically good.

This is the point of focus for the two serious problems presented in this chapter. Those problems both concern limit cases: cases where both beliefs are as well or poorly supported as possible. But limit cases are certainly not, it seems to me, the only points at which the evidential and likelihood of truth theories go wrong. They also wrongly count as equally epistemically good many cases where two believers have evidence which supports their beliefs to an equally moderate degree. In each of the following four cases involving pairs of evidentially equivalent beliefs, it seems to me that one of the beliefs is clearly epistemically better.

Case 1: Clair the clairvoyant is aware that her beliefs about future political assassinations are reliable – she has had many, the formation of all of them has involved a distinct phenomenology, and they have all been right. Now she believes that politician A is about to be assassinated. Dirk the detective shares her belief, but has come to it by dint of impeccable detective work.

It seems to me that there is no bar to supposing that Clair and Dirk's evidence supports their beliefs to just the same degree. When they are evidentially equivalent, I'm inclined to think that Dirk's belief is still *more of a cognitive achievement*, and so is epistemically better. It may not be epistemically better than Clair's would be, if Clair's belief were better supported by her evidence. But it is epistemically better than Clair's is, when their evidence supports their beliefs equally well.

This case suggests that, in addition to evidential support, cognitive achievement matters to our ordinary epistemic evaluations. But the case is also underdescribed, and so is very sensitive to theoretical biases. Committed evidential theorists, for instance, could simply insist that there must be a difference in evidential support, if indeed there is a genuine difference in epistemic value. Alternatively, it's possible that a truth-monist could give an account of the epistemic value of cognitive achievement. Virtue epistemologists, for instance, might give an account of this in terms of the greater *praxical* epistemic value of Dirk's belief. For Dirk's epistemic success is determined by his agency more than Clair's is.[172] So this case may be suggestive, but it is far from conclusive.

Case 2: Christy the cryptographer breaks the code of Sy the scientist's journal, and by so doing discovers a theory Sy has developed. In addition, she discovers that Sy's theory predicts that p, and comes to share much of Sy's evidence that p. If there is a lingering evidential difference between them, we can suppose that Christy also has some evidence bearing on p that Sy doesn't have, perhaps the testimony of other scientists. So we can ratchet up the quality of Christy's

---

seems to me that a plausible truth-monist response to the lottery paradox would be to abandon precise accounts of confirmation and thresholds for justification, but to preserve the basic motivation for truth-monism. The cases I present seem to me to strike instead at the basic motivation for truth-monism. But there is no room here for substantive consideration of the lottery paradox.

172 This would be a development, albeit a natural one, of the views in Greco 2009 and Sosa 2003.

additional evidence until Sy's and Christy's beliefs that p are equally well-supported by their evidence. And by adjusting the difficulty of the code and the research that went into Sy's theory, we can make their cognitive achievements of equal praxical epistemic value.

Nonetheless, it seems to me that Sy's belief that p is epistemically better than Christy's. It is, after all, better integrated into the rest of his beliefs – all the beliefs that went into and came out of the development of his theory. If you wanted to know why p was true, wouldn't you prefer to be able to ask Sy rather than Christy, even keeping in mind that Christy read Sy's journal and so shares much of the evidence that bears on why p is true? And, provided that we fill out the details of Sy's theory to make it suitably central to his field, doesn't the basis of Sy's belief that p seem *deeper*? The case suggests that something like Sy's depth of understanding makes a difference which is partly independent of how well his evidence supports his belief.

Case 3: Matt the mathematician comes up with a proof of p that is simpler and more elegant than the standard proof in the textbook, and from precisely the same axioms. But his proof is no more *valid* than the proof in the textbook. And it's from the same axioms, so it's sound if and only if the other proof is.

It's hard to understand how there could be a difference in evidential support between Matt and students who learn the proof in the textbook. And it's hard to understand how there could be a difference in praxical value between Matt's belief that p and the belief of the person who came up with the proof in the textbook. Can't we suppose that in fact it took the original prover much more work to discover the proof? Nonetheless, Matt's proof would be a better proof.[173] And, it seems to me, that proof is quite likely to make Matt's belief that p epistemically better than other beliefs that p. If you had the intuition that Sy's belief is deeper, doesn't *clarity* of the evidence for p also make an epistemic difference which is partly independent of evidential support?

Case 4: Suppose Renee has reached reflective equilibrium about her moral beliefs, while Inez has judgements about particular cases which are inconsistent with her more general beliefs. But suppose that both of them have equally good evidence that some particular action is wrong.[174] Perhaps Inez has additional evidence that bears on the facts of the particular case, for instance evidence that bears on what the foreseeable consequences of an action were, while Renee has slightly better evidence bearing on whether that kind of action is morally wrong. Moreover, we can specify that Inez has come by the facts of the case through considerable cognitive effort, equal to the cognitive effort involved in Renee reaching reflective equilibrium. Still, mightn't Renee's belief be epistemically better than Inez's? Doesn't reflective equilibrium add to the credentials of Renee's belief that p, just as independently of evidential support as the depth of Sy's reasons and the clarity of Matt's?

These cases are offered here only to bring out some intuitive reasons for dissatisfaction with the evidential and likelihood of truth theories of epistemic value. My intuitions about evidential support, like most people's, are highly sensitive to the details of cases like these, and it would be ideal to have cases which were even slightly less underdescribed. But filling the cases out seems

---

[173] Perhaps being better as a proof also contributes to the praxical value of Matt's belief. But insofar as Matt's performance is better, it's hard to understand the performance as better *for reaching the goal of truth*. Full discussion of this aspect of Matt's case would take us far afield into a discussion of praxical value.

[174] Depending on your moral epistemology, of course, that may be 0. If the example works at all, though, it should work whatever your views on moral epistemology.

fruitless without equally well worked out accounts of evidential support, or likelihood of truth – and those accounts have not been forthcoming. So, in the rest of the chapter, I will shift gears to present cases where our intuitions are less sensitive to unspecified details.

I.   Foley Cases

The first of these challenges comes in the form of Richard Foley's argument that reasons for belief are not always determined by one's evidence, as it might seem.[175] Foley's basic idea is that a proposition p may be supported by one's evidence, but one may nonetheless lack epistemic reason to believe it, because one knows that *if* one comes to believe p, it will be unlikely to be true. In Foley's example, you have excellent evidence that you will pass an exam. But you also know that if you believe that you will pass the exam, then the examiners will try to teach you humility by making the exam so hard that it is unlikely you will pass.

Why does Foley think that in this situation you would lack epistemic reason to believe p? Consider each of the three possible outcomes. If you disbelieve p or suspend judgement about p, then you will be disbelieving or suspending judgement about something which you know is likely to be true. On the other hand, if you believe p, then you will be believing something which you know is likely to be false. So you will either be suspending or disbelieving something which is likely to be true, or believing something which is unlikely to be true. So, Foley concludes, you lack reason to believe p, although your evidence supports it.

Although this is not the use to which Foley puts the case, it may seem to present a challenge to the evidential theory. Isn't this a case where it would be bad to believe something your evidence supports? So it seems like a clear counterexample to the evidential theory.

But it is not. In cases like this, your total evidence (i) supports p, but *also* (ii) supports the conditional that if you believe p, then p will be false.[176] So your evidential support for the truth of the proposition p comes apart from your evidential support for the truth of your belief that p – that is, the truth of the proposition p *if you were to believe it*. This is unusual. And because this is so unusual, when we talk about evidential support for your belief, we usually say simply that your belief is supported by your evidence if your evidence supports the truth of the proposition which you believe. But these cases show that this common way of talking about evidential support for beliefs is not quite right. So the evidential theorist should respond to the apparent counterexample by clarifying their account.

How, exactly, should they modify their account? To respond to the counterexample, they should explain the epistemic badness of your potential belief that p by citing the second fact about your evidence – (ii). The most conservative way to do this would be to say that a lack of evidence supporting the truth of your belief is of epistemic disvalue. Only slightly less conservatively, they might say that a belief is epistemically better (ceteris paribus) if the truth *of the belief* is better

---

[175] Foley 1992, pp. 27-30.
[176] I say "cases like his" because Foley underspecifies the case. Even if you have *some* evidence that p, as he specifies, that doesn't mean your total evidence supports p. In general, the evidence of believers will support that, if their total evidence supports that p, then they believe p (let this conditional be r). Since in this case you also have evidence that supports that if you believe p, then ~p, you have some evidence which supports that p, some that supports that if p then r, and some that supports that if r then ~p. In that case, I take it, your *total* evidence can't support either p or r. So Foley's case must be a case where your evidence does not support that if p, then r – that is, that if your evidence supports p, you believe p.

supported by your total evidence.

But your evidence also supports the truth of the proposition p, according to (i). And we might wonder whether believing a proposition, when your evidence supports the truth of the proposition but not the truth of the belief, is epistemically better than believing a proposition when your evidence supports neither. I am inclined to think that evidential support for the truth of propositions, when that comes apart from evidential support for the truth of the belief, does not make beliefs in those propositions any better, in general.

In one special version of the Foley case, evidential support for a proposition may coincide with epistemically better beliefs. But in this version of the Foley case, it is not the evidential support for the proposition which explains why the epistemically better beliefs are epistemically better.

Suppose someone in a Foley case is unaware of what their evidence supports, and in particular is unaware that their evidence does not support the truth of their belief that p. And they go on to form the belief that p, by reflecting on the evidence which supports the proposition. It may be that, if their ignorance of what their evidence supports is epistemically blameless, then the belief they form is epistemically better than it would have been if had they not had any evidence supporting the proposition. But it seems to me that cases like this are explained by a more general fact: cognizers who are blamelessly ignorant of what their evidence supports may form epistemically better beliefs than if they understood what their evidence supported, and formed the unsupported belief anyway. So this kind of case does not require taking evidential support for the truth of the proposition to explain epistemic evaluations. Rather, it supports taking blameless ignorance to exculpate beliefs which are better based than they might be.

These special versions of the Foley case aside, believers are generally aware that their evidence does not support the truth of their belief. And in Foley cases where believers are aware that their evidence does not support the truth of their belief, the fact that their evidence supports the truth of the proposition simply seems irrelevant to the epistemic goodness of their belief. If in these more usual versions of the Foley case you adopted the belief that you would pass the exam, that belief seems no better for being in a proposition which was supported by your evidence.

Why is support for the truth of the proposition irrelevant? Well, consider that your evidence might support the truth of many other things which are irrelevant to the epistemic status of your belief. For instance, your total evidence might support that ~p, but also support the conditional that if Zsa Zsa Gabor believes p, then p is true. But the fact that your evidence supports the truth of Zsa Zsa Gabor's belief is irrelevant to the epistemic status of your belief. And support for the truth of a proposition, when that comes apart from the truth of your belief, seems just as irrelevant. Why would the truth of the proposition be any more relevant in such cases than the truth of Zsa Zsa Gabor's belief?[177]

So the evidential theorist should not stop with the conservative refinement of their account above. They should further refine their account to say that the *only* evidential support which makes a difference to the epistemic value of a belief is evidential support for the truth of that belief. So the

---

177 This comparison is not intended to be persuasive, by itself. For one thing, evidential support for the truth of your beliefs is much more closely tied to evidential support for the truth of the propositions you believe, than it is to evidential support for the truth of Zsa-Zsa Gabor's beliefs. The point this paragraph is supposed to dramatize is that, in those few cases where support for the truth of beliefs and propositions comes apart, it is hard to see why evidential support for the truth of the proposition believed would be relevant. If it made sense of any of our epistemic evaluations, of course, it clearly would be relevant. In the rest of this section I argue that it doesn't explain any of our epistemic evaluations. That argument is needed for this reflection to have any force.

refined simple evidential theory will say that a belief is epistemically better precisely when the truth of the belief is better supported by evidence. This is not to rule out more complicated evidential theories, of course. But they will be complications of the relation to evidential support of the truth of the belief – not complications which change the relatum to the truth of the proposition.

An objection to this further refinement bears consideration. In positive versions of the Foley cases, evidential support for the truth of the proposition may seem to explain the epistemic badness of some beliefs.

In positive Foley cases, although you have excellent evidence that you will fail an exam, you also know that the examiners will make the exam impossible to fail, if you believe that you will pass it. So your total evidence supports ~p, but also supports the conditional "if I believe that p, then p." In that case, your total evidence supports the truth of your potential belief that p, but not the truth of the proposition. Still, the objection would go, there seems to be something epistemically worse about these beliefs than other equivalently well supported beliefs. Since there is by hypothesis no lack of support for the truth of the belief, a lack of support for the truth of the proposition must explain the belief's epistemic badness – or at least, that's what the evidential theory should say.[178]

Why does your potential belief seem epistemically bad? Compare this positive Foley belief with another belief whose truth depends on being believed: "this proposition is believed by me." From what state could you come to believe this self-referential proposition? If you didn't already believe it, then your evidence did not support the truth of your potential belief at the time when you came to believe it. What recommends the belief, when you are in the position of not yet believing it? Likewise, one might wonder: what recommends the belief that p in the positive Foley case, if you don't already have it? The parallel suggests a diagnosis. Both the positive Foley belief and the self-referential beliefs seem to be badly based. There is something suspect about basing your belief that p on evidence which supports that p will be true if you believe it.

This diagnosis is borne out by a further case, which we might call the inverse positive Foley case. This case differs from the positive Foley case in that, instead of your evidence supporting that you will fail the exam, your evidence supports that you will pass the exam – albeit very weakly. As in the positive Foley case, your evidence also strongly supports that if you believe you will pass, then you will pass. In this case, suppose you adopt a belief that you will pass. But your reason for adopting that belief is that it will be true if you believe it. You do not believe you will pass because of the evidence which supports that you will pass, independently of your believing that you will pass.

If this diagnosis is right, then there is a disanalogy between the original Foley case and the positive Foley case. In the positive Foley case, there is some inclination to think that a belief that p would be epistemically better than disbelief. So there is a question about the basis of the belief. On the other hand, in the original Foley case, there is no tendency to think that you should adopt a belief that you will pass. So there is no question about the basis of a belief – suspension and disbelief need not have the same kind of basis as beliefs.

It seems to me that, in this case, you would go wrong in just the same way that your belief goes wrong in the positive Foley case, and in the self-referential belief case. Your belief is poorly

---

178 Another way for the evidential theorist would be to point out that in cases where you evidence supports the conditional "if I believe that p, then p," the belief you form has less praxical value. After all, intuitively, it wasn't much of an achievement that you got it right. But this would be a hard case for some accounts of praxical value. For you have got it right through your own cognitive agency, rather than by chance or luck. After all, it is the fact that you believe it that makes it likely to be true!

based. But in this case, unlike the others, your total evidence *does* support that you will pass. So the explanation of the disvalue in all three cases is not that your evidence fails to support the proposition that it will pass. Instead, the explanation of the disvalue of the belief is in terms of a problem with the basis of your belief.

What is the problem with the basis of your belief, in all these cases? The most conservative proposal to handle these cases would say that a belief that p is epistemically better, ceteris paribus, if it is based on evidence that is independent of its being believed than if it is based on evidence which is dependent on its being believed. That rules out evidence which supports that if you believe p, p will be true. And it explains the fishiness of positive Foley cases. But, crucially, it does not take evidential support for the truth of propositions to be of epistemic value, when that comes apart from the truth of beliefs.[179]

The upshot is of this challenge, then, is a constraint on plausible evidential theories of epistemic value. Only evidential support for the truth of *beliefs* matters. When evidential support for the truth of your belief that p comes apart from evidential support for the truth of the proposition that p, evidential support for the truth of the proposition is irrelevant to the epistemic status of the belief.

For the sake of brevity and clarity, I've avoided explicit consideration of the likelihood of truth theory in this section. But I hope it is clear that everything said about degree evidential support in this section could equally well be put in terms of likelihood of truth. What matters is likelihood of the truth of *beliefs*, rather than likelihood of the truth of propositions. Both these restrictions will matter when we come to discuss the third problem.

II. The Preface

The preface paradox presents a very difficult kind of problem. For on some versions of the preface, it involves a rational belief which is both unlikely to be true and poorly supported by your evidence: roughly, the belief that all of the claims one makes in a book are true and that at least one of them is false.

This belief is, in fact, so unlikely to be true that you can easily come to know *a priori* that it is false. And this fact allows us to bypass some hairy questions. It allows us to bypass questions about how to calculate likelihoods, and it allows us to bypass questions about thresholds – how likely the truth of a belief must be in order for the belief to be epistemically good. We can bypass these questions because of the following principles.

(APFL)   If S knows *a priori* that her belief that p is or would be false,
         p is maximally unlikely for S.

(APFE)   If S knows *a priori* that her belief that p is or would be false,
         then S's total evidence maximally countersupports p.

Does the preface paradox really involve an epistemically good belief which we can

---

179 Is this a proposal that a truth-monist could make or accept? Yes, they could. The intuitive strangeness of the move for a truth-monist is that, if *truth* is all that matters in epistemology, what does it matter whether the truth of the belief is partly dependent on its being believed? But, of course, TM allows that different relations to the truth count differently. So there is no reason why a truth-monist could not complicate their theory in this way.

nonetheless know a priori to be false? In short, no.

There are strong and weak versions of the paradox. In the weak version, we assume only that (i) the author of a book may rationally believe each of the claims she makes in the book, $\{B_1..B_n\}$, but also (ii) rationally believe a claim she makes in the preface, B0, that not all of $\{B_1..B_n\}$ are true. But (iii) B0 is inconsistent with the conjunction of claims in $\{B_1..B_n\}$. So (iv) the author might rationally believe each of the inconsistent set $\{B_0..B_n\}$. This is the conclusion of the weak version of the paradox. The strong version assumes in addition that (v) if she rationally believes each claim she makes in the book $\{B_1..B_n\}$, then she rationally believes that all of $\{B_1..B_n\}$ are true - that is, ~B0.[180] So (vi) she rationally believes B0 & ~B0 - a patent contradiction.[181]

Thus the strong version of the preface does involve a rational belief – the belief that B0 & ~B0 – which the author can easily know *a priori* to be false. According to APFL, this is a counterexample to the likelihood of truth theory. And according to APFE, it is a counterexample to the evidential theory.

However, there are serious worries about the principles of conjunction which would support (v). For my part, I find these worries compelling. You may rationally believe all the claims in the book separately, but that does not mean you may rationally believe the conjunction of all those claims. So, although (vi) would involve a counterexample to both the evidential and likelihood of truth theories, it seems false. Why does it seem false? For precisely the reason the evidential theorist should cite – that your total evidence can't support a contradiction, because no body of evidence can support a contradiction.[182]

So the conclusion of the strong version of the paradox is unproblematic, because it is very plausibly false. What about the conclusion of the weaker version of the paradox, i.e. (iv)? Unfortunately, (iv) does not hold the same promise that (vi) does. In (iv) there is no single proposition believed and known *a priori* to be false. And, crucially for the purpose of arguing against the likelihood of truth theories, each of the beliefs in $\{B_0..B_n\}$ may be likely to be true, provided that n is larger than two.[183] And there seems no bar to thinking that your evidence may support the truth of each of the claims in an inconsistent set, individually.[184]

Thus the preface paradox does not provide compelling grounds for rejecting the evidential and likelihood of truth theories of epistemic value. For those, we will have to turn to Moore's

---

180 The precise content of this belief, in discussions in the literature, depends on the closure principle for rational belief which the author favors - but these fine shades of difference won't matter for my purposes here.
181 Scrupulous readers will note that there's a distinction between have two beliefs, one in B0, and the other in ~B0, and having one belief in a patent contradiction. Thus, strictly speaking, the inference to (vi) is invalid. But the distinction doesn't matter for my purposes here, and the closure of rationality of belief under conjunction which licenses (v) is generally taken to be unrestricted, so that one can also conjoin rational contradictory beliefs. That is, practically speaking, (vi) will be admitted to follow from (v) if (v) is admitted.
182 Perhaps this also means that your evidence can't *include* a contradiction. A full defense of either of these claims would take us far beyond the scope of the present section. The point is that this requirement is so plausible that, as an argument against the evidential and likelihood of truth theories, this one seems like a very long shot.
183 Assuming that the threshold of rational belief is likelihood of truth = ½. More carefully: $n > (1 - 1/t)$, where t is the threshold of evidential support for rational belief. For more detailed discussion of the weak version of the paradox, and a Bayesian interpretation of it which would be friendly to the likelihood of truth account, see Hawthorne & Bovens 1999.
184 Though this is not obvious. In fact, Evnine 2001 and Ryan 1991 both argue against (iv), and their arguments, if successful, would generalize to the claim that your total evidence cannot support each member of *any* inconsistent set. In this context, that argument would throw the problematic baby out with the bathwater, though – the evidential theorist could say that evidence and epistemic value go together whether or not Evnine and Ryan are wrong.

paradox.

III. Moore's paradox: some inexplicable epistemic evaluations

G.E. Moore noticed that in general there would be something odd about asserting "it's raining, although I don't believe that it's raining," although that might very well be true.[185] This has come to be known as Moore's paradox. Moore's paradox seems to hold some promise in an argument against the evidential and likelihood of truth theories of epistemic value. The third-person version "it's raining, but he doesn't believe it" is often well-supported by evidence, and likely to be true. But intuitions that it would be epistemically bad to believe "it's raining, although I don't believe that it's raining" run deep.

These propositions – I'll refer to them as MPs, for Moore's Paradoxical propositions – have received significant scholarly attention, but a compelling account of why it would be epistemically bad to believe them has not materialized. Some accounts appeal to dubious constraints on belief to explain their epistemic badness.[186] Others cite formal properties of MPs which are not unique to MPs but are shared with preface propositions like B0 above.[187] Yet other approaches simply fail to explain all the relevant data about irrationality, either because they take irrationality to be sensitive to the order of the conjuncts when it clearly is not,[188] or because all they give is an account on which MPs are necessarily irregular, infrequent, and "estranged."[189] I won't here go into the details of these accounts here, except where they help me make out the challenge to the evidential and likelihood of truth theories.[190] What matters for present purposes is simply that there is no compelling account ready to hand, with which the evidential and likelihood of truth theories might be patched up to handle the problems I'll discuss.

Before developing those problems, we'll need to get much clearer on MPs. First of all, what counts as an MP? Which propositions are in the relevant way like "it's raining, although I don't believe it?" Unfortunately, the task of demarcating the class of MPs is closely bound up with what one thinks is wrong with believing or asserting the paradigm case. And it seems likely to me that there are both multiple interesting classes of propositions which are all interestingly like that paradigm case, as well as multiple problems with asserting and believing the paradigm case.[191]

In this chapter, I will only be concerned with two of these classes. These classes of MPs are marked out by their form, and differ only in the scope of the negation. Omissive MPs, or OMPs for short, put the negation outside the belief operator and so are of the form "p & ~Bp", where "Bp" abbreviates the specifically first-person "I believe that p." These are omissive in the sense that they involve the epistemic sin of *omission* of belief in p. If, instead, we put the negation inside the belief operator, we get commissive MPs, or CMPs for short: "p & B~p." These are commissive in the sense that they involve an epistemic sin of commission, namely believing ~p.

---

185 Moore 1944
186 Most notably: Hintikka 1962, Shoemaker 1995, de Almeida 2001, Kriegel 2004, Williams 2004.
187 Sorenson 1988.
188 Gillies 2001.
189 Moran 1997 & 2001.
190 A brief summary of approaches may be found in Green & Williams 2007b, pp. 15-22.
191 Green & Williams 2007b also give a helpful survey of demarcational questions and issues; Sorenson 1988 gives an entertaining and more wide-ranging account of how to demarcate MPs, though he is driven by an account of what's wrong with the paradigm case which leads him astray, for reasons to be explained in the last section of this chapter.

Among many facts about MPs, there are three facts which are of particular concern here besides the fact that MPs may be true. One is that there is something epistemically less than ideal about believing any MP. The second is that CMPs may be truly believed, and they may also be arbitrarily well-supported by evidence and arbitrarily likely to be true. OMPs, on the other hand, are like Foley cases in that, although they are possibly true, they cannot be truly believed – this is the third fact.

In the next section I argue that this third fact is problematic for the evidential and likelihood of truth theories, because the epistemic value of beliefs in OMPs vary, even when they are maximally unlikely to be true, and maximally countersupported by one's evidence, according to APFL and APFE. In the final section of the chapter, I argue that the second and first facts hold. If either of these arguments are right, then the evidential and likelihood of truth theories get the extremes of epistemic value wrong: they wrongly count as equivalently extreme some cases of varying epistemic value.

IV. "p but I don't believe it" – Omissive Moore's Paradoxical propositions (OMPs)

OMPs, of the form "p but I don't believe p," cannot be truly believed. If I believe an OMP, then I believe the first conjunct. So, if I believe an OMP, then I believe p. But this proposition, i.e. Bp, is only true if the second conjunct of the OMP, i.e. ~p, is false. It follows from the fact that I believe an OMP that my belief is false.

More precisely: assuming that belief distributes over conjunction (BDOC),[192] it follows from $B(p\&\sim Bp)$ that $\sim(p\&\sim Bp)$. Suppose for reductio that an OMP is truly believed:

1. $B(p\&\sim Bp) \& p \& \sim Bp$ [assumption for RAA]
2. Bp [1, BDOC, & elim]
3. $\sim Bp$ [1, & elim]
4. $Bp \& \sim Bp$ [2,3, & intro; RAA]

If someone runs through this argument, and knows BDOC *a priori*,[193] then they will know a priori that their OMP belief is false.[194] According to APFL, these beliefs will all be maximally unlikely to be true. So, according to the likelihood of truth theory, these beliefs will all be maximally epistemically bad. Similarly, according to APFE, these beliefs will all be maximally countersupported by their evidence. So, according to the simple version of the evidential theory, these beliefs will all be maximally epistemically bad. Any case of varying epistemic value among the

---

192 BDOC: $B(p\&q) \rightarrow Bp \& Bq$.
193 Why think BDOC is knowable *a priori*? Because, plausibly, what it is to believe a conjunction is just to believe the conjuncts and to understand in addition the relation between them. The inverse principle, $Bp \& Bq \rightarrow B(p\&q)$, is false precisely because believers often don't "put two and two together" - or, in this case, they don't put p and q together. Readers who doubt that BDOC is knowable *a priori* may reformulate the APFL and APFE principles in other terms, for instance, by substituting "at the center of the web of belief" for "*a priori*" both in those principles and in the claim BDOC is knowable *a priori*.
194 Since all I need here is one counterexample, I'm suppressing several complicating factors which may occur to scrupulous readers. Some readers of the reductio may doubt the validity of reductios. Some readers might be confused and think *this* reductio is invalid, though they think reductios in general are fine. The possible cavils are probably without limit. But let us simply stipulate that they are not true in the cases we're interested in, even if this necessitates a move from the Churchlands to the Schmurchlands, who by stipulation do not doubt the validity of reductios.

OMP beliefs of those who have run through this argument, then, will constitute a counterexample to these theories.

Caution is in order, here. For it might be that OMPs cannot be truly believed because they cannot be believed at all. On one interpretation, this is precisely what Wittgenstein thought. But his reason for thinking that they are impossible to believe, on this interpretation, is the implausible claim that utterances of "p" and "I believe that p" are semantically equivalent,[195] which no-one would now endorse.

Besides, it seems clear that there are definite ways to talk yourself into believing OMPs. Consider that, if it's not *obvious* that there are any such things as beliefs, it seems clear that reflecting on that lack of obviousness in a rainstorm might be articulated by observing that[196]

(NO)   It's raining, but it's not obvious that I, or anyone else for that matter, *believes* that it's raining.

Moreover, given certain evidence – e.g. whatever evidence eliminative materialists like the Churchlands take to support their view that there are no beliefs – I might move on from merely entertaining the proposition that I don't believe that it's raining, to positively disbelieving it. I might first come to believe:

(NB)   There are no beliefs

And by reflecting on both NB and the continuing rainstorm, I might then come to believe an OMP:

(OMP1)   It's raining, but I don't believe that it's raining.

So, if it's not obvious that there are any beliefs at all, it looks like one could believe OMP1, because one might *think* that one had evidence which supported that belief. That is, one might think that one's evidence supports NB, and so one might think it supports the particular instance of NB expressed by the second conjunct of OMP1.[197] So OMPs can in some situations be believed, albeit only falsely.

These same situations give us counterexamples to the simple evidential theory. For it seems clear that some OMP1 beliefs will be better than others, even for believers who run through the reductio above. Compare, for instance, the OMP1 belief that the Churchlands might form, with the OMP1 belief of someone who has just read the Wikipedia entry on eliminative materialism. Even after they run through the reductio, it seems clear that the Churchlands' beliefs are epistemically better: more respectable, more informed – they demand to be taken seriously in a way that the Wikipedia reader's belief does not. But, according to APFE, once the Churchlands have run through the reductio, their beliefs are equally poorly supported by their total evidence. So the simple evidential theory wrongly counts them as equally epistemically bad. And the same argument, using

---

[195] See Malcolm 1995, Wittgenstein 1958, section II.x, pp. 190e-192e, and Wittgenstein 1980, §471-504.
[196] For this example and consideration of some others like it, see Hajek 2007.
[197] There are many ways to take yourself to have evidence in support of an OMP1 belief. One might fail to distinguish between evidential support for the proposition NB (which, let us suppose, you have) and evidential support for the belief. Or one might make that distinction but fail to realize its normative import, because one hasn't considered Foley cases. Or one might make that distinction, realize its normative import, but fail to consider the reductio. And given humans' marvelous cognitive dexterity, there are surely many other ways, too.

APFL instead of APFE, will work for likelihood of truth theories.

Nor will it help to move to the more sophisticated evidential account from the first section – the one that adds a basing relation. For we can simply suppose that the Churchlands and the Wikipedia reader base their belief on their evidence. The problem is not with the basis of the belief, but with their evidence. According to APFE and APFL, their evidence is equally bad: in both cases it maximally *countersupports* the OMP1 belief. So this case is a counterexample to the more sophisticated evidential account, too.

Is there *any* way to defend the insight behind the evidential and likelihood of truth views? In the next chapter I'll propose an amendment to them that will handle this case. But one might want to resist these apparent counterexamples with a less radical change than I propose there. A few objections in particular bear consideration, though there is no way to anticipate every possible objection or response to the apparent counterexamples.

One thought is to make out the difference in terms of exculpation. Just as some beliefs in Foley cases are better than others because the believers are blamelessly ignorant of what their evidence supports, one might think that the Churchlands are blamelessly ignorant of what their evidence supports. There are probably many ways to develop this idea, but the common problem, it seems to me, is that the Wikipedia reader will also be blamelessly ignorant – or can be made to be, by refining the case. And if both the Churchlands and the Wikipedia reader are blamelessly ignorant of what their evidence supports, then their beliefs will both be exculpated.

Another objection might try to make out the *praxical* value of the Churchland's belief. But the intuitive idea behind praxical value is measuring the skill of a performance as a cognizer. Suppose that we put the Churchlands in the place of Sy the scientist in case 2 from section 1 above. And suppose the cryptographer breaks the code to their journals – in this imaginary situation, they have authored the same research, but instead of publishing their research, they have secreted it away in their journals. It seems as if the cryptograper's performance involves just as much skill. And if praxical value is instead supposed to be the value of achieving success through one's own agency, it's hard to see why the Churchlands must exceed the cryptographer in that case, either.[198]

A different and more serious objection picks up on something counterintuitive about saying that the Churchlands' evidence supports their belief just as badly as the Wikipedia reader's. For APFL and APFE also imply that their evidence is equally bad for NB. That is counterintuitive. If the Churchlands' evidence doesn't support their NB beliefs any better than the Wikipedia reader's evidence supports their NB belief, what have the Churchlands done all that research for? Hasn't some of it produced some considerations in favor of their belief? So there must be something wrong with APFE and APFL.

The basic problem may seem to be with having evidence for the truth of a *belief* in NB. After all, it's not surprising that no body of evidence can support the truth of NB *if believed*, for roughly the same reason that it seems like no body of evidence can support a contradiction. For if NB is believed, then NB is false. Nonetheless, evidence can support the truth of the proposition

---

[198] A twist on praxical value would locate the value of the Churchland's beliefs in their being surrounded with other beliefs about the subject matter which are well-supported. For instance, the Churchlands will have well-supported beliefs about why some objections to eliminative materialism fail, while the Wikipedia reader will not. The difficulty with this response is to make out why that adds to the value of the particular belief in question. I do not think the difficulty is insuperable – in fact, this is one thing which contributes to what, in Chapter 5, I will call the discursive epistemic value of the Churchland's belief.

NB. The obvious suggestion is that the Churchlands' evidence better supports the truth of the proposition NB, and so better supports the truth of the proposition OMP1. And it is this fact about evidential support which explains why the Churchlands' beliefs in OMP1 are better.

But in the Foley case in section I, evidential support for the truth of the proposition to be believed did not seem to make a belief any epistemically better. So it's simply not true that evidential support for the truth of the proposition to be believed makes a belief epistemically better. For this reason, while I am sympathetic to the idea that the Churchlands' evidence is better, I do not think this proposal is the right way to make out *how* it is better. In Chapter 5, I'll return to the question of whether the Churchlands' evidence is better.

In the earlier discussion, I suggested that evidential support for the truth of the proposition to be believed, when that comes apart from evidential support for the truth of the belief, is simply irrelevant to the epistemic status of the belief. It is no more relevant to the epistemic goodness of your belief than evidential support for the truth of Zsa Zsa Gabor's belief is relevant to the epistemic goodness of your belief. What matters to the epistemic status of your cognitive state is evidential support for the truth of your cognitive state.

But in the Churchlands' case, of course, it might be that they have a *different* cognitive state which is better off: the successor cognitive state (SCS for short) which we are often in when our folk theory ascribes a belief. The SCS will be a non-propositional attitude, of course. For this reason, it is not clear just what it could mean for the Churchlands' evidence to support the *truth* of an SCS. But put this worry aside, and assume that the Churchlands' evidence does support the truth of their SCS which they give voice to by asserting NB. Could that fact explain the epistemic betterness of their belief?

I think not. The crucial point is that we need only a single case for a counterexample, and this response simply pushes the problem back. For we could simply run the same kind of case substituting SCS for belief. Suppose there are some researchers who come to be in the SCS that there are no such things as SCSs, and take themselves to have evidence for that SCS. Those researchers could then adopt an SCS of the non-propositional form "p and I don't have an SCS that p."[199] And in the Wikipedia of the future, there might be an entry which bowdlerized their evidence for denying the existence of SCSs. But wouldn't the researcher's SCS be epistemically better than the Wikipedia reader's SCS?

So this proposal pushes the problem back, from a comparison between a Wikipedia reader's belief and the Churchlands' belief, to the comparison between a Wikipedia reader's SCS and some other possible researcher's SCS. But we still have a counterexample to the evidential theory and the likelihood of truth theory. I suspect that this proposal gains some plausibility from the thought that my claims about evidential support for NB are dialectically not kosher (if not quite question-begging) in an argument against the Churchlands. Perhaps that thought is right. But my point here is not that the Churchlands' belief *is* epistemically bad. My point is just that it is epistemically bad according to the evidential and likelihood of truth theories. And in this context, there is no reason to move to a more recherché counterexample, simply in order to be more charitable to the Churchlands.

Clearly this does not show that there is *no* way for the evidential or likelihood of truth theories to explain the epistemic betterness of the Churchlands' OMP1 beliefs. But the case resists easy solution, and seems to turn up a deep tension. On the one hand, there seems to be something

---

[199] p will, of course, not be a propositional variable here, but a variable ranging over whatever kind of content an SCS has.

epistemically good about all the cognition that goes into forming the attitude of skeptics about the existence of attitudes. But, on the other, no evidence can support the truth of an attitude which denies the existence of that kind of attitude!

V.   "p but I believe ~p" – Commissive Moore's Paradoxical propositions (CMPs)

Unlike OMPs, CMPs can clearly be supported by evidence, and not just in rare cases. Suppose that you think that your evidence supports ~p, and form a belief that ~p for that reason. In this case, it seems that your evidence supports that B~p. But, if your evidence actually supports p, then in general your evidence supports p & B~p.[200] Of course, in general it won't continue to support that CMP if you realize that your evidence supports p rather than ~p. But the point is just that your evidence can support a CMP.

Moreover, if the evidence that p in the situation envisaged above is not misleading, then p is true, as also is B~p. And surely it is possible that the evidence is not misleading. If so, it's possible for CMPs to be both evidentially supported and true. Of course, this doesn't show that they can be evidentially supported, true, *and* believed, all at the same time.

But CMPs, unlike OMPs, can be truly believed. As the following argument shows, however, they can only be truly believed if one has patently contradictory beliefs, that p and that ~p:

1. B(p&B~p) & p & B~p
2. Bp   [1, BDOC, & elim]
3. B~p   [1, & elim]
4. Bp & B~p   [2,3, & intro]

How can one have patently contradictory beliefs? I'll go into the possibilities in some depth, in order to anticipate the objection that one can't have patently contradictory beliefs at all, and so also can't have a true and evidentially supported belief in a CMP. There seem to be as many ways to have contradictory beliefs as there are ways to think that contradictory things are true, but there are two broad camps: one may take oneself to have evidence for each of the contradictories, or one of the contradictory beliefs may be resistant to evidence.

Taking yourself to have evidence for p and for ~p
There are also many ways to take oneself to have evidence for both p and ~p. One may have unusual beliefs about evidence, or one may not realize that p and ~p are contradictory, either because of odd beliefs about truth, or because of semantic ignorance.

For instance, one might think that in cases where *some* of one's evidence supports p, and a distinct part of one's evidence supports ~p, one's total evidence sometimes supports both p and ~p. I think this claim about evidential support is false, and pretty clearly false. But pretty clearly false does not mean unbelievable. And this claim about evidence does seem believable.

Or, if one thinks that there are truth gluts, then whenever one thinks that both p and ~p are true, one may have contradictory beliefs. Or if one thinks that truth is relative, but is wrong about that, then one might in general have contradictory beliefs when one thinks that p (relative to r) but

---

[200] In general, but not always, because even when one is mistaken about what one's evidence supports, the truth of these may not be sufficiently independent for the evidence which supports p and supports B~p to also support p & B~p.

~p (relative to r').[201] Or, even if one is not wrong in general that truth is relative, one might still think that it is relative in some particular case where it is not, or think that the truth of some claim is relative to different things when in fact it is relative to the same thing. For instance, one might be the wrong stripe of subjectivist about beauty, even if beauty is relative to *something*.

Or one might fail to realize that two sentences determine contradictory propositions, as Kripke's Pierre, and so take one body of evidence to be relevant to "Londres n'est pas jolie" and another body of evidence to be relevant to "London is pretty."[202]

Evidence-resistant beliefs
Another way to have contradictory beliefs would be to be in the position of Barry Stroud's skeptic about colors or values, who believes that there are no colors (or values), but is also committed to the existence of colors (or values) by some other beliefs, which are nonetheless not *evidence* that there are colors (or values) – for instance, in the case of values, by believing that others' actions are intentional. In that case, the skeptic's belief that there are values is not rationally responsive to the skeptic's evidence against it. Let p = that there no are colors. Then the skeptic's evidence supports p, and for that reason the skeptic believes p. But the skeptic also has a belief that ~p which is not sensitive to the evidence that p, in the sense that although he believes that ~p, the skeptic fully appreciates that his evidence supports that p, and does not support ~p. So the evidence of the rational skeptic who has read and been convinced by Stroud thus supports the CMP that there are no colors and that she believes that there are some colors.

Or take beliefs one ascribes to oneself only as a result of psychotherapy. Suppose that, as a result of psychotherapy, I come to attribute to myself Bp, where p is, e.g. that spiders are scary, or that my father hated me. That I fully appreciate the evidence for ~p does not in these cases undermine my confidence that I believe p, since that is based on, for instance, the necessity of attributing that belief to me in order to explain my behavior. So, in this situation, my evidence supports a CMP, in the one case that spiders are not scary, but I believe they are, and in the other case that my father didn't hate me, although I believe he did. And there seems to be no bar to those CMPs being true, as well. So CMPs can be true, supported by evidence, and believed, all at the same time.

Even if the CMP is false, because one lacks the contradictory belief that ~p, one can still have evidence that supports p & B~p. Suppose that any of the scenarios described above is actually impossible. Still, it's not impossible that one's evidence could support that one was in one of those scenarios. And in that case one's evidence would support p & B~p. Moreover, and very importantly, it doesn't seem like there is any bar to that evidence supporting p & B~p to as high a degree as it could support any p.

What's epistemically wrong with believing true and evidentially supported CMPs?
Given that they can be supported by evidence, and true, one might think that there's nothing wrong with believing a CMP. And I don't disagree that one might have a justified belief in a CMP, and perhaps even know it, under those circumstances. But that doesn't entail that there's nothing wrong with believing a CMP, in the sense that no negative epistemic evaluations are true of it.[203] In

---

201 This is true of relativism in general, but whether it's true of a particular theory will, of course, depend on that theory; for instance, this may not be possible on a theory on which truth is believer-relative.
202 Kripke 1979.
203 Though perhaps it does entail that such CMPs would be *blamelessly* believed; but blameless belief does not exhaust

particular, even if two beliefs are justified, one may be *less* well justified than the other.

And this is precisely the position of a belief – any belief – in a CMP. Although it may be arbitrarily well-supported by evidence, and may be true, it can't be as epistemically good as possible:[204] a belief that it's raining, if maximally well-supported by evidence, is epistemically better than a belief that it's raining but I believe it's not raining, even if that belief is also maximally well-supported by evidence. After all, believing a CMP ensures a lack of coherence among one's beliefs: such a lack of coherence that for the first several decades of discussion the aim of scholarly debate was to give an account of why, despite often being true, MPs were either unassertable or unbelievable.

The question, then, is whether the evidential and likelihood of truth theories can give an account of the epistemic badness of CMPs, including those which are maximally well-supported by evidence and maximally likely to be true. They might, for instance, advert to Sorenson's account of "belief-based criticism." Sorenson's idea is that a flaw in your cognitive system is *due to* the presence of the MP belief. So, he says, an agent S is subject to belief-based criticism if S would have inconsistent beliefs if three conditions were satisfied: (i) S believes that p, (ii) p is true, and (iii) S is an absolutely thorough believer, in the sense that her beliefs are closed under entailment and material implication.[205]

But Sorenson's account of belief-based criticism doesn't capture his idea of a flaw due to a certain belief. An agent is subject to belief-based criticism when there's a flaw in her cognitive system, regardless of where the blame should fall. So, for instance, an agent will be subject to belief-based criticism if, out of epistemic modesty, she believes EM:

(EM) At least one of my other beliefs is false

However, it seems clear that beliefs in EM, rather than being the source of a cognitive flaw, will generally involve a recognition of flaws in one's cognitive system. So belief-based criticism will not distinguish between beliefs in EM and beliefs in CMPs, although beliefs in EM seem clearly to be epistemically better than beliefs in CMPs.

The problem is not simply that we need a better way to capture Sorenson's intuitive idea that the MP belief is somehow the source of the flaw. For a true and maximally well-supported CMP belief may not be the source of the cognitive flaw. The source of the flaw might be an evidence-resistant belief, for instance. Once one is saddled with an evidence-resistant belief, adopting a CMP seems like a recognition of that specific cognitive flaw, in the same way that EM is a recognition of a more general cognitive flaw.

Nor is there any other obvious way to discriminate between CMPs and EM. The difference may seem to be in what the believer knows about *which* beliefs are false. Minimal reflection will reveal to a believer of a CMP that either their belief that p or their belief that ~p is false. On the other hand, EM provides no clue whatsoever about which of my other beliefs are false. So one might try to discriminate between EM and CMP beliefs on the basis of the size of the set of beliefs

---

epistemic value.
204 If you think that beliefs in contingent propositions can never be as epistemically good as beliefs in necessary propositions, add the qualification "for a contingent proposition" to one or both of these claims: CMPs can be arbitrarily well-supported by evidence up to the limits of evidential support for contingent propositions, but can't be as epistemically good as possible for contingent propositions.
205 Sorenson 1988, p. 39.

impugned: the smaller the set, the worse.

But it is not the sheer size of the set of impugned beliefs which matters. For one thing, this predicts distinctions between different people's beliefs in EM which don't seem matched by intuitions about epistemic goodness. But an EM belief seems to be just as epistemically good for the most skeptical human, with relatively few beliefs, as it is for the most credulous and profligate human believer.[206]

For another thing, the size of the set of beliefs is not the only variable which seems to matter. Consider Crimmins' case,[207] in which a trustworthy friend, whom I know to be smart, tells me that I know him under a different guise, and under that guise I believe him to be an idiot. Now, if I know only one person to be an idiot, then I would simply revise my beliefs about that person: the person I thought was an idiot was just my friend, pretending to be an idiot. Now, suppose that we fix the size of the set of beliefs impugned in this case, so that in a 2-Crimmins case it might be my beliefs that {Abe is an idiot, Bea is an idiot}, and in a 3-Crimmins case, it might be my beliefs that {Abe is an idiot, Bea is an idiot, Cesia is an idiot}. And we can do the same with CMPs, so that a 2-CMP belief, like $\sim(p\&q)$ & $B(p\&q)$, will impugn $\{p, q, \sim p, \sim q\}$. So a 3-Crimmins case will be worse than a 1-CMP case, a 5-Crimmins case will be epistemically worse than a 2-CMP case, while a 2-CMP case will be worse than a 3-Crimmins case. But it seems clear both that we do not have these detailed intuitions, and that there are other factors which matter, such as the obviousness of the inconsistency between p and $\sim$p, and the difficulty of recalling each belief that someone is an idiot.

Some CMPs, then, are counterexamples to the evidential and likelihood of truth accounts as stated. They may be maximally well-supported by your evidence, and maximally likely to be true. A CMP belief may be based on this maximally good evidence. And yet the beliefs are not maximally epistemically good.

What could they be lacking? Praxical value in this case doesn't seem to be any help. Nor are there any other obvious candidates. The evidential fault seems to lie somewhere in the formation of the contradictory beliefs required for the CMP to be truly believed. But the CMP need not inherit that evidential fault. So the prospects for fixing up the evidential theory seem dim.

In the next chapter I describe a way to handle these cases which is natural and plausible, but which makes a fundamental change to the evidential and likelihood of truth theories of epistemic value.

---

[206] Perhaps this is an overstatement: perhaps the most skeptical human's EM belief would be *slightly* less epistemically good. But I think we can still make out the point, which is that the sheer size of the impugned set does not matter, by comparing instead those whose thought ranges more widely. Couldn't such a person have more beliefs, but EM would be no epistemically better for them than it would be for an equally careful thinker whose investigations were more narrowly circumscribed?

[207] Crimmins 1992.

Chapter 5: Discursive Epistemic Value.

In Chapter 3 I argued that the two best truth-monist accounts of epistemic value were the evidential theory and the likelihood of truth theory, but then in Chapter 4 I argued that neither of those theories is adequate. There are some epistemic evaluations which neither theory explains. So what does explain those epistemic evaluations?

In this chapter I explain them in terms of some of the same kinds of persuasive power which make knowledge worth wanting. In the first section of the chapter, I set out some intuitive motivation for this account of what I'll call discursive epistemic value, along with some intuitive problems. In the second and third sections of the chapter, I make the account of discursive epistemic value more precise and make clear how it avoids all but one of the problems of the first section, as well as how it handles the serious problem cases and the intuitively dissatisfying cases from Chapter 2. In the fourth section, I respond to the lingering problem: what makes discursive epistemic value count as epistemic?

In the final section of the chapter, I consider how discursive epistemic value fits with the evidential and truth-likelihood theories of epistemic value. Discursive epistemic value cannot on its own be a replacement for those theories, that much is clear. Instead, discursive epistemic value can be compounded with the best account of other epistemic evaluations. In particular, it could be added to either an evidential theory or a likelihood of truth theory. But it is unclear whether the compound theory that would result would be a more complicated monist theory, or a pluralist theory of epistemic value. I suggest that this is because of divergent motivations for having a monist theory in the first place. Some motivations for truth-monism are satisfied, or at least not clearly violated, by the compound theory. But insofar as truth-monism is motivated by the thought that epistemology is all about getting the truth, and not about interacting with others, this will not be a truth-monist theory.

I.   Motivation & Problems.

Two problem cases from Chapter 4 show that the evidential and likelihood of truth theories get the margins of epistemic evaluations wrong. They wrongly count some beliefs which are not maximally epistemically bad as maximally epistemic bad, and they wrongly count some beliefs which are not maximally epistemically good as maximally epistemically good. I'll quickly review those problem cases in this section, and an intuitive solution to them will guide the rest of the chapter.

The first case involves getting the margins of the epistemically worst beliefs wrong. These theories treat beliefs in omissive Moore's paradoxical propositions (henceforth "OMPs"), of the form "p but I don't believe p," as all maximally bad. But there is intuitively quite a bit of variation among such beliefs. The Churchlands, for instance, could have OMP beliefs which seem better than others. After all, they believe:

(NB)   There are no beliefs

But their belief in NB seems clearly epistemically better than, say, the belief of a student who reads a bowdlerized summary of the Churchlands' views on Wikipedia and adopts NB for that reason. And that disparity in epistemic status would transfer to OMP beliefs that both the Churchlands and the student might form by reflection on NB.

But, if the argument of Chapter 4[208] is right, then that disparity in epistemic status is not a matter of likelihood of truth or support by total evidence. After all, the disparity in epistemic status would persist even if the Churchlands and the student were shown that OMP, like NB, can't be both true and believed by them, in which case there would clearly be no disparity between their beliefs with respect to likelihood of truth or support by their total evidence.

So what else could make the Churchlands' OMP beliefs better than others? One clear difference lies in what they can say to support their OMP beliefs. To justify each OMP belief, they'll cite their evidence for p, of course, but also, and crucially, they'll cite what they take to be evidence for NB. Then they'll justify NB by citing what they take to be evidence for it. The Wikipedia reader, on the other hand, will offer a less good defense of NB, and so of OMP.

Now, in general, what you can say in support of your belief is a matter of producing evidence which shows that those beliefs are likely to be true. But, again, if the argument in Chapter 4[209] is right, then these beliefs are equally poorly supported by the believer's total evidence, and they are equally unlikely to be true. So the epistemic differences between the Churchlands' and the Wikipedia readers' OMP beliefs are not due to differences in how well their total evidence actually supports what they believe. Instead, the epistemic differences between them must be due to something else about how the Churchlands could support their OMP beliefs.

It might be thought that what the Churchlands can say in support of their beliefs is simply a reflection of some more important facts about what they *think*. For instance, the Churchlands think that they have evidence which supports their view. But, of course, so may the Wikipedia reader. And it seems clear that this wouldn't make the Wikipedia reader's beliefs epistemically equivalent. Nor, in general, are beliefs made epistemically better by the presence of a second-order belief that evidence supports them. For instance, the beliefs of skeptics who view the evidential support of their beliefs with a jaundiced eye are generally better than the beliefs of the less critical, even when the skeptics more accurately and pessimistically assess the evidence they have for those beliefs.

Although the Churchlands and the Wikipedia reader might have the same second-order beliefs about their evidence, the Churchlands would clearly be better people to talk to about NB. So it looks as if it is really something about what the Churchlands can *say* in defense of their beliefs, and not what they think about them, which makes their OMP beliefs epistemically better. That is not to say that what they think does not matter at all. Of course, what the Churchlands can say in support of their belief will be intimately connected to what they think about it. The point is that we can use the clear advantage the Churchlands have, namely their ability to speak in defense of their belief, to identify what it is about their thought which is good.

What precisely is it, about the Churchlands' ability to speak in defense of their beliefs, which is *always* epistemically good? That's the subject of the next section. For now, I'll just give it a name: discursive epistemic value.

Discursive epistemic value also holds some promise for dealing with the second kind of problem case from Chapter 4. In those cases, beliefs in commissive Moore's Paradoxical propositions (henceforth "CMPs"), of the form "p but I believe ~p," are maximally well-supported by one's evidence, and maximally likely to be true, but are still less than maximally epistemically good. They are also epistemically worse than beliefs in propositions with similar formal properties, such as "I have at least one other false belief." So truth-monism also gets wrong the upper margins

---

208 Chapter 4, section IV.
209 Chapter 4, section V.

of epistemic evaluations.

Naturally, much ink has been spilled in an attempt to explain what would be epistemically bad about believing a CMP. Unfortunately, the extant accounts of the epistemic badness of CMP *beliefs* are inadequate.[210] But the original paradox raised by Moore[211] was to explain why CMPs would be bad to *assert*, rather than why they would be bad to believe. And accounts of their communicative badness are better. So it would be nice if these accounts could be somehow extended to explain not only the badness of asserting CMPs, but also the epistemic badness of believing them. If there is something epistemically good about being able to speak in defense of your beliefs – if, that is, there are some discursive epistemic values, then those discursive epistemic values might bridge the gap between communicative badness and epistemic badness.

And there does seem to be something odd about the justificatory ability of someone who asserts a CMP. They assert a conjunction of the more general form p & Bq. Normally, someone who asserts a conjunction of this form would be taken to put their weight behind both p and q. But in a CMP, where q is the negation of p, this means that the speaker puts their weight behind two contradictory claims: p and ~p. So they are in an unusual justificatory position with respect to the CMP. Even those who trust them, and would normally adopt a belief that p based on their testimony that p, will be unlikely to adopt a belief in the 3rd-person counterpart of what they've asserted (i.e. "p and he believes ~p").[212]

It's not obvious that the oddness of that justificatory position involves a specifically *epistemic* fault of the CMP belief. But the problem in Chapter 4 seemed to be specific to CMPs. And the obvious candidates for an epistemically significant property which is also specific to CMPs have already been ruled out in Chapter 4. So it is worth looking for a less obvious epistemically significant property which is specific to CMPs. The oddness of the justificatory position seems like a promising candidate on both counts. And if it is, then we can give a unified account of the OMP and CMP cases from Chapter 4: the problematic betterness of the Churchlands' OMP belief is a matter of the Churchlands' better justificatory position, and the problematic worseness of CMP beliefs is a matter of a CMP believer's worse justificatory position.

That is not to say that it is obvious how to bridge the gap between the badness of asserting and the badness of believing a CMP. Accounts of the badness of asserting CMPs don't extend straightforwardly to the epistemic badness of believing them. For instance, Moore's own account, and many since, begin by observing that an assertion that p *expresses* a belief that p. Thus when asserting a CMP, of the form p & B~p, one asserts that one has one belief, that ~p, while *expressing* a belief that p. So even though one does not assert that one has contradictory beliefs, one simultaneously does two things which are in conflict: asserting B~p and expressing Bp. The problem with extending accounts like this to explain the epistemic badness of believing a CMP is that it is not clear what the analogue of "expressing a belief" could be, for belief. Moore and others postulate that asserting p represents me as believing p. But believing p does not represent me as being a particular way, and so *a fortiori* does not represent me as believing p. So it's not obvious how to carry out what seems initially to be a promising application of accounts of Moorean assertion.[213]

---

210 For a very quick survey of extant accounts and problems, see Chapter 4, section III.
211 Moore 1944.
212 In other ways the justification of a CMP will be atypical, too. It will, for instance, involve two very different and mostly disjoint bodies of evidence in support of each conjunct. But this atypicality looks more like an effect of the strange kind of conjunction a CMP represents – most possible conjunctive beliefs would differ from people's actual beliefs in this way.
213 Pagin 2008 makes this criticism of applying standard accounts of Moorean assertion to Moorean belief.

Along with the promise of discursive epistemic value, however, come some problems. The most pressing among them is to figure out precisely what discursive epistemic value could be. Many factors contribute to how well someone can justify a particular belief, and at least some of them do not contribute to its epistemic standing. Some people are simply more glib than others, but more glib people do not generally have epistemically better beliefs. Conversely, some people have trouble articulating the careful reasoning on which their beliefs are based, but their beliefs are not for that reason epistemically worse. So an account of discursive epistemic value must somehow screen off factors that contribute to justificatory ability but which, like glibness, make no contribution to epistemic goodness. In section II, I'll formulate an account of discursive epistemic value which screens off the obvious non-epistemic factors of discursive abilities.

Even an account which does successfully screen off factors which are clearly epistemically irrelevant, and so captures something about our ordinary epistemic evaluative practices, must still say something about why these discursive values count as specifically *epistemic* values. Our ordinary epistemic evaluative practices, after all, might be somehow mistaken. For instance, one might want to admit that some pragmatic features of a context – say, the importance of getting it right whether p – influence our ordinary epistemic evaluations of beliefs that p. But one might then want to deny that this aspect of our ordinary evaluative practice reflects anything about what is of epistemic value.[214] I'll call this worry the "discursive encroachment" worry, since it parallels the "pragmatic encroachment" worry discussed in Chapter 1. I'll return to it in section IV.

II. Discursive Epistemic Value & the Churchlands' OMP beliefs

If discursive epistemic value is supposed to capture something epistemically good about the Churchlands' ability to say things in support of their OMP beliefs, the simplest account of discursive epistemic value would simply try to generalize from that ability:

(DV1)   S's belief that p is of positive discursive epistemic value iff S can defend p

This, of course, won't give us a full account of discursive epistemic value. For one thing, DV1 doesn't say anything about comparative claims between two things which do have positive discursive epistemic value. DV1c gives us those comparative judgements:

(DV1c) S's belief that p is of discursive epistemic value commensurate with S's ability to defend p

One shortcoming of the DV1s, of course, is that it's not clear what counts as defending p. But set that aside for the moment. The DV1s reveal more precisely one of the serious worries from section I. Many factors are relevant to whether S can defend p which nonetheless seem irrelevant to whether S's belief that p is epistemically better than it otherwise would be. Among other things, DV1 overestimates the link between discursive epistemic value and a smooth tongue, to paraphrase Williamson.[215] And it does so because it relativizes discursive epistemic value to an individual agent's discursive abilities. So it implies that the discursive epistemic value of someone's beliefs is determined, in part, by their elocutionary ability.

---

[214] I discuss pragmatic encroachment in Chapter 1, section II.
[215] Williamson 2000, p. 258 (footnote 10). Williamson is commenting on Brandom's account of warranted assertion.

But what's remarkable about the defense the Churchlands could give of their OMP beliefs isn't their ability to speak, or to speak eloquently. It's not how they would speak. Rather, it's *what* they would say. Using that content to defend OMP beliefs would have epistemic value even if it were spoken by someone radically different in expressive ability and with very different background beliefs. It would have that epistemic value even if for some reason the believer were struck dumb, and unable to articulate any defense at all.

Focusing on what the Churchlands are able to say, rather than how they would say it, makes clear one way to screen off obviously epistemically irrelevant discursive abilities, like whether someone can speak, or whether they can speak well. The account of discursive epistemic value must be reformulated in terms of whether one proposition counts as a defense of another:

(DV2) S's belief that p is of positive discursive epistemic value iff
there is some q which is a defense of p, and S is in a position to cite q as a defense of p.[216]

And we can give the comparative account in terms of the quality of the defense:

(DV2c) S's belief that p is of discursive epistemic value commensurate with
the quality of the defense of p, viz. q, which S is in a position to cite as a defense of p.

The DV2s solve one problem, but they leave us with the problems of understanding what it is for one proposition to be a defense for another, and how to measure the quality of a defense. The first step in solving that problem is an easy one. Well-defendedness is a matter of evidential support relations between propositions.[217] One proposition is a defense for another if the one is evidence for the other, and being a better defense is a matter of being, in some sense, better evidence. But evidence that is better how?

Well-defendedness is a matter of having influential evidence

At this point, it may be helpful to remember why the Churchlands' OMP beliefs are not supported by their evidence, since having a well-defended belief may now sound very much like having an evidentially supported belief. But remember that what matters to whether one's belief that p is supported by evidence is whether one's *total* evidence supports the truth of p *if believed*. That's not true in the Churchlands' case, at least after they run through the reductio which shows that no OMP belief can be true.[218] So the Churchlands' belief is not supported by their evidence. Nor are others' OMP beliefs, once they have run through and understood the reductio.

Although the Churchlands' total evidence does not support the truth of their OMP *beliefs*, they do have some evidence which supports the truth of OMP *propositions*. And one might think that it is this fact – simply the fact that they have this evidence – which makes their beliefs epistemically better than the Wikipedia reader's. But in Chapter 4 I argued that, where evidential

---

[216] In general, q will be a long conjunction. In the case of the Churchlands' OMP beliefs, it will consist largely of the conjoined assertions in their relevant published work relevant to NB, plus their evidence for the first conjunct, p, of the OMP belief.

[217] Instead of evidential relations between p and q, a likelihood of truth theorist will want to substitute confirmation relations, or some other probabilifying relation. For the sake of brevity, I'll only consider an account of well-defendedness in terms of some facts about evidence. But everything I will say could equally well be put in terms of facts about confirmation or probabilification.

[218] For which see Chapter 4, section V.

support for the truth of p comes apart from evidential support for the truth of p if believed, the fact that an cognizer's total evidence supports the truth of p is epistemically neutral. It would not make believing p epistemically better than suspending judgement that p. So the fact that the Churchland's total evidence supports the truth of OMP propositions won't explain why the Churchland's OMP beliefs are better than the Wikipedia reader's.

Another way to make out how the evidence which the Churchlands have might contribute to the epistemic goodness of the belief would be to restrict the evidence which is relevant. If their *total* evidence doesn't support the truth of their OMP beliefs, and the fact that their total evidence supports those OMP propositions is epistemically irrelevant, then perhaps what matters is that some *fragment* of their total evidence does support the truth of their OMP beliefs. There is, I think, something right about this. But it won't do, as it stands. For there will frequently be fragments of one's total evidence that support the truth of things one *knows* are false. That fact would not make a belief in those propositions any better. More carefully and generally: whenever p supports r, but the conjunction of p & q strongly countersupports r, and I believe both p and q, then in general my belief that r would be no epistemically better because I believe p. But p could be a fragment of my total evidence. So, clearly, the mere fact that *some* fragment of one's total evidence supports the truth of a belief isn't epistemically good.

What is special, then, about the fragment of the Churchland's evidence which does support the truth of their beliefs, and so makes their beliefs epistemically better than the Wikipedia reader's? Certainly it is true that they have put more thought into their position. But it seems clear that putting thought into a position doesn't always result in epistemic betterness. Instead, what matters is that the fragment of the Churchlands' evidence which best supports the truth of the belief (which will include their published work, but omit the reductio)[219] meets certain standards: it is evidence which is publishable in reputable scholarly sources; it addresses objections; it is a well-worked-out view; it has to be taken seriously. But, at the same time, it is not obvious, nor even generally believed.

There are many possible ways to spell out what lies behind these positive evaluations of the fragment of the Churchland's evidence that supports OMP beliefs. Of these, the one that seems most plausible to me is that the Churchlands' evidence is more likely to affect how strongly other people's evidence supports NB and so OMP beliefs.[220] Someone who reads and understands the Churchlands' writings has better evidence for her OMP beliefs than someone who hears and understands what the Wikipedia reader has to say in defense of NB. Of course, once she runs

---

[219] Omission of the reductio is crucial. The principles in Chapter 4 depend on taking the reductio to be part of the Churchlands' total evidence. Nothing about those principles entails that the Churchlands' total evidence, prior to running through the reductio, fails to support the truth of their OMP beliefs. So, by taking a fragment of their evidence which omits the beliefs they acquire after running through the reductio, we get a fragment which supports their OMP beliefs as well as it did prior to running through the reductio. Perhaps it is also hard to understand how their evidence could support their OMP beliefs even prior to running through the reductio. For present purposes, I assume that it can. If it can't, that would by itself be a significant problem with the evidential theory, since presumably going through the reductio does or at least could make a difference to the epistemic value of the Churchland's OMP beliefs.

[220] Another possibility, which seems less plausible, is that what matters is how well their evidence would have supported their OMP belief prior to going through reductio. It is plausible that this would distinguish the Churchlands and the Wikipedia reader. But it's hard to see how this kind of counterfactual could generalize without overgenerating epistemic value. After all, most people have beliefs which their evidence would have supported much better if they hadn't come to have some conflicting evidence. But how does that make their beliefs better, once they have the conflicting evidence?

through the reductio, her evidence will no longer support her OMP beliefs. Nonetheless, the Churchlands' evidence is better than the Wikipedia reader's.

Better how? In short: more influential. But this does not mean just that the Churchlands' evidence *is* likely to change others' minds. It means that the Churchlands' evidence is likely to make a difference to what others' evidence supports. Influential evidence, in this sense, is what it takes to have a well-defended belief. And more influential evidence will make for a better-defended belief:

(WDc) A defense of p, i.e. q, is good to the degree that q is more likely to make other relevant cognizers' evidence support p better than it otherwise would

It is hard to say precisely which cognizers are relevant. If all possible cognizers were relevant, then WDc would count all evidence as equally uninfluential. So that clearly would not capture the right idea. But any restriction can look like chauvinism. If, for instance, we restricted the class to other actual cognizers, or to cognizers in the same culture, or who speak the same language, then how influential some body of evidence was would be too sensitive to accidental features of actual people, cultures, or languages.

If p belongs to a fairly distinct field of inquiry – if it is a proposition which can only be expressed in English by using the technical jargon of some specialized theory – then the class of cognizers who matter for whether q is influential evidence for p might be composed of those who study or work in that field. That would be a decent first pass at capturing what we mean when we say that ideas or experts are influential.

This might make for a somewhat parochial notion of influence, however. Darwin's ideas are influential, for instance, precisely because they have had an effect not just on biologists and students of biology, but because they have spread widely outside of biology. So what is important about students and those who work in a field? One thing is that they are generally held to some standards of reasonable belief. Another is that they generally have an interest in the truth of propositions which touch on their field of study or work. So we might broaden the class of cognizers relevant to having influential evidence for p, by including anyone with a serious interest in getting p right,[221] and who is in addition a responsible believer.

This will narrow the class of relevant cognizers sufficiently to give WDc evaluable content, on which it is plausibly true and applies to the problem cases from Chapter 4. A more precise account would of course be better. But there will be many questions about making the account precise which would require in depth discussion that is not required for the proof of concept I'm aiming to give, here.

For instance, we might also want to add a restriction on relevant cognizers, to the effect that their empirical evidence must have significant overlap with the cognizer giving the defense, in order to prevent favoring beliefs with less empirically falsifiable content. Or we might not. In deciding, we can take as a guide our intuitions about what evidence *we* have to take seriously, and then asking who the relevant cognizers would be, who would make that evidence influential according to WDc.

The strategy of using these intuitions as a guide to the relevance of cognizers also helps answer another pressing question. Should only *actual* cognizers count? If so, then epistemic values would be overly sensitive to seemingly irrelevant facts about which cognizers were alive. If a freakishly specific plague wiped out all the academic mathematicians, that would change some facts about which evidence was influential. For instance, the epistemic value of the mathematical beliefs

---

[221] That is, with an interest in believing p if p is true, and disbelieving it if p is false.

of those who majored in math as undergraduates might suddenly go up. This seems odd, even if we reflect that these math majors also now count as the experts. So it seems clear that some non-actual cognizers must count as relevant. And we can keep applying this strategy until our account of which cognizers count as relevant is in reflective equilibrium with our intuitions about epistemic value in particular cases.[222]

Before moving on with this rough and ready handle on the relevant cognizers, it may be helpful to consider a parallel with an earlier claim about the epistemic goodness of evidential relations. In considering Foley cases in Chapter 4, however, I suggested that facts about the support your evidence gives to propositions you might believe is irrelevant to epistemic value in the same way that facts about the support your evidence gives to Zsa Zsa Gabor's beliefs is irrelevant. Isn't WDc just taking account of *many* of these irrelevant facts about what your evidence supports? In short, no. How your evidence bears on any particular individual's beliefs is irrelevant to the epistemic value of *your* beliefs, because it is no measure of the quality of your evidence. On the other hand, how your evidence bears on the beliefs of many relevant cognizers *is* a measure of the quality of your evidence.

It is a measure of the quality of evidence which attempts to factor out peculiarities of your evidential situation, just as we might want to factor out a logician's scruples about some argument which would be enormously influential in another field. For instance, the fact that the logician does not accept the validity of some form of argument commonly thought to be valid does not detract from the publishability or importance of an argument she might give with that form, though it will detract from how well the argument supports *her* belief in the conclusion. That is a peculiarity of her evidential situation. And that peculiarity need not bear on how influential the argument is.

How discursive epistemic value explains the problem cases & intuitively dissatisfying cases from Chapter 4.
DV2c and WDc together give us an account that applies straightforwardly in the case of the Churchlands' OMP beliefs. Their beliefs are much better defended than the Wikipedia reader's. So their beliefs are of greater discursive epistemic value. This is the case before they grasp the reductio, of course, but unlike what their total evidence supports, it is unchanged by running through the reductio.[223]

This case does not bring out the specifically discursive character of discursive epistemic value. For we could give roughly the same explanation of the Churchlands' OMP beliefs in terms of their *possessing* more influential evidence. That is, it looks like a fact about the evidence they have, that does the explanatory work, rather than their ability to cite it.

Simply having influential evidence, rather than being able to cite it, also seems to be crucial in three of the cases from the beginning of Chapter 4. Sy the scientist's evidence would be more influential because it is deeper than Christy the cryptographer's, some of whose evidential support for p is not part of a theory explaining why p is true, but is instead testimonial evidence. So there may be an objection to which Sy has a response, but Christy does not. Sy's evidence will be more influential because it may give these objectors a reason to believe p.[224] Similarly, Matt the

---

222 Thanks are due to John MacFarlane for pressing this worry.
223 Objection: what if all the relevant cognizers had run through the reductio? Reply: this is a place where the charitable interpretation of the Churchlands matters. If all the relevant cognizers had run through the reductio for *belief*, their evidence might still support the truth of the SCS in an OMP. For the argument that this move doesn't solve the problem for the evidential and likelihood of truth theories, see Chapter 4, section IV.
224 Objection: what if Sy's explanation is beyond most people's capacity to understand? Isn't it possible that his evidence would then be *less* influential than Christy's testimonial evidence? Reply: If most of the relevant cognizers

mathematician will be able to convince some responsible cognizers who found the old proof too difficult to follow, so that his better proof for p amounts to more influential evidence for p. And Renee, by virtue of reaching reflective equilibrium, will have more influential evidence for her moral beliefs because her evidence that p will make others less likely to succumb to casuistry than inconsistent Inez's better supported beliefs about the non-moral facts of the case.

Of course, in most cases the ability to cite influential evidence will go together with having influential evidence. But in the other case from the beginning of Chapter 4, an ability to cite influential evidence comes apart from simply having influential evidence, and it is the ability to *cite* influential evidence which seems to matter. In that case, Clair the clairvoyant's belief seems epistemically worse than Dirk the detective's. DV2c gives us an account of why. Clair can, of course, cite some evidence. She can cite the fact that she has an experience of a certain phenomenological character which has been reliably correlated with correct beliefs about political assassinations in the past. But her evidence is not open to inspection in the same way that Dirk's is. Dirk can show you his evidence; Clair cannot simply show you her experience. She has, instead, to testify about it. You have to trust that Clair is telling the truth about her experience, and this means that the evidence she can cite will be less influential than Dirk's evidence. That is not to say that Clair *has* less influential evidence, however. If someone else simply had Clair's experience – that is, if it were their clairvoyant experience, rather than hers, they would be able to eliminate the possibility of lying that comes with testimony.

A unified account of all the cases from Chapter 4 is a mark in favor of a theory of epistemic value. By taking the important fact about the Churchlands' evidence to be what they *cite* rather than simply what they think, the present account gives such a unified account. That is a mark in favor of the present account, and in addition bears out the intuition mentioned earlier, that what makes the Churchlands' OMP beliefs epistemically better is a fact about what they can *say* in defense of their beliefs.

Worries about discursive epistemic value.

Does discursive epistemic value on this account overgenerate predictions about epistemic goodness? It seems to me that it does not. Believing p when you have more influential evidence for p is epistemically better than believing p when you have less influential evidence for p. Of course, in a typical case, when you are a typical believer, this will coincide with an increase in the support for p afforded by your total evidence. But even when those two factors come apart, as in the Churchlands' case, having more influential evidence for a proposition makes your belief in that proposition better.

While there is no way to rule out all potential counterexamples, at least one worry demands a response. It might be said that in the Foley cases you have influential evidence that you will pass the exam. Your evidence is exactly the sort that many people's beliefs that they will pass exams are grounded on. So retailing that evidence for them would make their total evidence support the belief that you will pass the exam. But that fact seems to count for nothing, epistemically speaking. Your influential evidence that you will pass the exam would not render epistemically better a belief that you will pass the exam.

---

would be so confused by Sy's explanation that it did not improve their evidential support for p, then it's not clear to me that Sy's evidence is really better than Christy's. But the relevant cognizers need not be the same class for all propositions. And, in particular, it seems likely that the relevant cognizers for determining whether Sy's evidence for p is influential are the other experts whose testimony Christy relies on. These cognizers will not generally be confused by Sy's evidence, if it is any good at all.

There is a way in which this is clearly right: your influential evidence that you will pass the exam does not make *believing* that you will pass the exam epistemically better than *suspending* belief about whether you will pass the exam. But this is not a counterexample to the claim that the – clearly epistemically bad – belief that you will pass the exam is epistemically better than one supported by less influential evidence. Indeed it seems to me true that a belief that you will pass the exam would be epistemically better than a belief which had less influential evidence going for it, in the same odd situation. In one case your evidence is better than the other, even though it is undermined in both cases.

This response gives rise to another worry. If the discursive epistemic value of your belief in the Foley case can't make it worth believing, that suggests that discursive epistemic value is *merely* evaluative. That is, discursive epistemic value has no role to play in giving advice about what to believe, and no bearing on one's deliberation about what to believe.[225] The thought is that the normative question in epistemology is "what should I believe?" And it looks like discursive epistemic value is simply irrelevant to that question. So discursive epistemic value seems to be something that, while it may help explain our evaluative practice, does not matter at all for our cognitive lives, and is not something for which we should strive.

But shouldn't we strive to have and cite evidence that is more open to public inspection, and strive also for deeper reasoning, better proofs, and reflective equilibrium? Even if those traits by themselves never settle the question of what you should believe, they certainly seem relevant to the question of how you should be cognitively. So it seems to me that this worry understands epistemic advice too narrowly. Sure, good advice about what to believe is exhausted by facts about what your total evidence supports, as is good advice about what to suspend belief concerning, and what to disbelieve. But these are not the only questions about how we should be, cognitively. We might also give advice about *how* to be in that state. Should you be in a belief state with more influential evidence, or less influential evidence? It seems to me that you should be in a belief state with more influential evidence.

So discursive epistemic value is not merely an evaluative standard, but is relevant to giving advice about how to be, cognitively speaking. It is simply relevant to the more general question: "how should you be, cognitively?" rather than simply to the more narrow question "what should you believe?" We are apt to overlook this more general question, I think, because it is so rare for evidential support to be tied, and discursive epistemic value functions as a kind of tie-breaker, when evidential support is tied.[226]

III. Discursive Epistemic Value & CMP beliefs

On this account of discursive epistemic value, what matters is what you have to say, and not your ability to say it. And what matters about what you say is that it constitutes influential evidence, in the sense made more precise by WDc. It is on this latter ground that CMP beliefs fail. The evidence for CMPs is always going to be less influential than it could be, because it is always to some degree self-undermining. After all, some bits of the evidence provided will point against what, as a whole, the evidence provided supports. In this section, I develop this thought and respond to an objection to it.

---

[225] Thanks are due to Niko Kolodny for pressing the first part of this worry.
[226] Thanks are due to John MacFarlane for this helpful formulation of the point.

In Chapter 4, the problematic fact about CMPs was that even when your total evidence supports them maximally well, they aren't maximally epistemically good. Now, if your total evidence supports a CMP maximally well, then some fragment of it supports that CMP maximally well, since some of your total evidence will be irrelevant to that CMP. So the problem with cases like this can't be that you don't have a fragment of evidence which supports the CMP, and supports it maximally well.

But that fragment of evidence is necessarily not maximally influential. Let p be a CMP, of the form p1 & I believe that ~p1, and let q be the fragment of your evidence that supports p. If q were maximally influential evidence for p, then there would be no pair of propositions (p', q') such that q' is *more* influential evidence for p' than q is for that CMP.[227] But for every CMP, there is such a pair. Simply let q' = the minimal fragment of q which best supports p1. Then q' is more influential evidence for p1 than q is for p.

Why? Because q supports that I believe ~p1.[228] Now, for many cognizers, this will make no difference: they will take note that the evidence I've produced supports p1, and also supports that I believe that ~p1. But for some other cognizers, the support q provides for p1 will be impugned by the fact that q also supports that I believe ~p1. On the other hand, q' does not present this possibility to the audience. It supports p1 without supporting that I believe ~p1. That is, it does not present the evidence which some cognizers will take as conflicting evidence.

Now, there will always be cognizers with wacky background beliefs who take the evidence for conjunctions in wacky ways. The point here is not that we can dream up such wacky background beliefs in this case. The point is that there are always going to be more cognizers than usual – perhaps with less wacky background beliefs than usual – who take the evidence for CMP beliefs to be at least partially self-undermining. This captures something natural, I think. If Abe asserts a CMP, and produces some evidence that p and some evidence that he believes ~p, one very natural question for Abe is: but why do you believe ~p? And that is a question which wouldn't be asked of most bodies of evidence which support p. For many of these hearers of a CMP who wonder "but why do you believe ~p?" the CMP will be less well supported by q than p is by q'. Thus a CMP will always be supported by less influential evidence than p, its first conjunct.[229] So, by WDc, a CMP will always be supported by less than maximally influential evidence. So, by DV2c, a CMP will always be less than maximally discursively epistemically good.

On the other hand, the epistemic modesty belief

(EM)   At least one of my other beliefs is false

may be supported by maximally influential evidence. For one thing, it's not clear whether the evidence for EM is self-undermining. But even if that evidence *is* self-undermining in a way parallel to CMPs, EM can still be supported by maximally influential evidence. For the evidence for EM is

---

227 A wrinkle, here, to do with maximal support: we have to pick p and p' so that "maximal support" determines the same level of support in both cases. But this amounts to a bare existence claim: for each p, there is some p' which has the same level of maximum support as p. That seems very plausible.

228 This is *not* because, if q supports (p & r), then q supports p and q supports r. Rather, it's because of facts specific to CMPs: to end up having maximally good evidence for believing it, your evidence that you believe that ~p must be fairly independent from your evidence that p.

229 A parallel argument might also show that the second conjunct of a CMP will also be in this position, of always being supported by more influential evidence than the CMP itself (when they are both supported by one's evidence). Nothing follows from anything here about whether the first conjunct is supported by more influential evidence than the second conjunct (or vice versa).

roughly similar across humans: so even if the evidence for EM in some way impugns itself, there is no systematically better alternative, in the way that p was a better alternative for each CMP. While the question "but why do you believe ~p?" is a natural and potentially embarassing question for someone who asserts "p, but I believe ~p," the question "but why do you believe any of the other things you believe?" is not a natural or potentially embarassing question for someone who asserts EM. EM is a fixed part of the evidential situation of fallible and self-aware cognizers; CMPs are not. So the evidence for EM should be maximally compelling to any human; not so, for CMPs.[230]

It's important to remember that we're talking about very special cases. My diagnosis of the badness of believing CMPs here is not intended to be a full diagnosis of what's wrong with them in a typical case. In a typical case, your evidence will not support that you have contradictory beliefs, and so your evidence will not support a CMP. In those cases, you would be wrong to believe a CMP because to do so would go against your total evidence. My claim here has just been that in the very atypical cases where your total evidence *does* support a CMP, there is still something wrong with believing it: it is not maximally discursively epistemically good.

IV. Discursive Encroachment?

On some accounts of epistemic justification, pragmatic factors make a difference to whether or not some beliefs are justified. For instance, the importance for S of getting right whether or not p is the case may determine the degree of evidential support which is required for a belief that p to be justified. On these accounts, whether a belief is justified is a function of two kinds of factor: one pragmatic, and one about evidential support.

One response to these accounts holds that of these two factors, only the one about evidential support is properly speaking an epistemic factor. If that means that only the fact about evidential support is a properly epistemic value, then it means that evaluations like "S's belief that p is epistemically justified," although they seem purely epistemic, would turn out to be a kind of hybrid.

Since, on my account, apparently epistemic evaluations are also a kind of hybrid, of evidential epistemic value and discursive epistemic value, one response to my account would be strictly parallel to Feldman's response to pragmatic encroachment.[231] It would say that the core epistemic values are the only ones which are properly epistemic. The evaluations which discursive epistemic values explain may be part of our ordinary epistemic evaluative practice, but properly speaking they are not epistemic.

An initial reply to this objection seems obvious. The proponents of pragmatic encroachment put forward a kind of factor which is clearly not the sort of thing epistemology has traditionally considered. In fact, pragmatic factors are frequently one of the explicit contrasts by which introductory epistemology students can be brought to an initial understanding of what it means to say that a reason is *epistemic*. On the other hand, I put forward a factor about the quality of the *evidence* someone possesses for their beliefs. Their candidate factor is something epistemologists have never looked into. On the other hand, my candidate is one that, if I am right, is central to what marks out the philosopher-king's knowledge in the *Republic*.[232] So the case against discursive epistemic value is at least not as strong as the case against what might infelicitously be called

---
230 Note that this distinction between EM and CMPs require that we understand the relevant agents in WDc to be finite, fallible and self-aware cognizers.
231 For Feldman's response, see Chapter 1, p. 4.
232 I argue for this in *The Stability of Knowledge*.

pragmatic epistemic value.

There is, however, a deeper worry. For, while discursive epistemic value is *one* way of measuring the quality of the evidence someone has for a proposition, it is hardly the *only* way to do that. And one might think that epistemology proper is essentially egocentric,[233] in the sense that the properly *epistemic* quality of your evidence supervenes on some facts about *you*, together with some facts about evidential relations, and some facts about the bit of the world your beliefs concern. But what gets signally left out of that list is facts about what would be good evidence for other people. And discursive epistemic value depends essentially on what would be good evidence for other people. So one might object that discursive epistemic value is not properly epistemic, because it is not egocentric. It has the wrong supervenience base to be properly epistemic.

But episteme is properly epistemic if anything is. And whether or not someone has episteme *does* depend on facts about other people. After all, Socrates repeatedly says that episteme is teachable, where that must mean that someone with episteme can teach others what they have episteme of. And Socrates' audience, in both the *Meno* and *Protagoras*, accept this claim without quibble: not as if Socrates is working with an unusual concept of episteme.[234] Besides, both wisdom and expertise seem like plausibly epistemic concepts. But they both imply being cognitively better in some way than other people: so the supervenience base of both includes the same sort of facts about other people that discursive epistemic value depends on. If epistemology *proper* has seemed to some to be egocentric, that seems to be at best a Cartesian misconception.[235]

If the account of discursive epistemic value given above is right, then one factor in the *epistemic goodness* of beliefs is also a factor in their goodness. For the ability to teach, which in Chapter 2 I argued is one reason why knowledge is good, is a kind of hybrid ability. It involves, of course, some pragmatic abilities which aid in communication. But it also involves communicating influential *evidence*, and I have argued in this chapter that having influential evidence to communicate is a special kind of epistemic good: it is discursively epistemically good.

V.   Truth-monism Reconsidered.

The theory of epistemic value I have argued for is compound. It builds on the evidential theory, which says that (i) beliefs are, ceteris paribus, epistemically better if they are based on your total evidence, and that total evidence supports them. To this it adds that (ii) beliefs are, ceteris paribus, epistemically better if they are of more discursive epistemic value.

This compound theory is not a truth-monist theory. But it is consistent with two motivations for truth-monism.

First, it is consistent with the demarcational motivation for truth-monism. The idea is that we will have no good way to demarcate which evaluations are properly epistemic, if not in terms of the special relationship to truth which evidence is supposed to have. The demarcational concern, I think, is misplaced: we have a firm enough grip on paradigm cases of justified belief. There are, of course, very serious disputes about justification, and partly for this reason it is difficult to use justification to draw a clear and precise demarcation. But, as I argued in chapter three, the clear and precise demarcation that truth-monists like Alston have offered throws the demarcational baby out

---

233 Foley's term, though not necessarily Foley's use of it.
234 I argue for this in *Knowledge is Teachable*.
235 Which is not to say that it's a misconception *Descartes* suffered from, but a misconception of those who treat epistemology as if it started with Descartes.

with the bathwater. And, besides, it's not clear why we need a clear and precise demarcation of the properly epistemic. Do we need a precise demarcation of the properly ethical? Why would we?

Even if the demarcational concern is well-motivated, and even if our grip on justification were not up to the job, it seems to me that our grip on evidence *is* firm enough to do the job. And discursive epistemic value is a matter of being able to cite influential evidence, which is in turn defined in terms of evidential support relations and other relevant cognizers. So discursive epistemic value does not muddy the demarcational waters, as it were. Epistemology is still all about evidential support relations.

Perhaps the demarcation of the properly epistemic may even be given in terms of standing in a relation to truth. For if evidence can indeed be accounted for in terms of truth, or if an adequate rational reconstruction of evidential relations can be given in the way the likelihood of truth theorist hopes, then discursive epistemic value is simply a more restricted relationship to truth.

On the same condition, the compound theory will be acceptable to a naturalist, provided of course that cognizers are. For the compound theory makes reference only to evidence, the cognitive act of citing evidence, and the other cognizers whose bodies of evidence matter to how influential one's evidence is. As I said in the Chapter 1, the prospects for a naturalistic account of evidence seem dim – but the present point is that they are no dimmer if we extend the evidential theory by adding (ii), above. So the compound theory is friendly to this second motivation for truth-monism, of giving a naturalistic theory of epistemic value.

Things look rather different, however, when we ask whether epistemology is all about truth, or whether that characterization is misleading. From this perspective, amending the evidential theory to include a basing relation is a kosher extension of the evidential theory only because it is another sense in which we are in a better relation to the truth. We aren't in a better relation to the truth by believing an additional truth, but by believing for the right reason. And epistemic goodness is all about being in a better relation to the truth.

In contrast to the inclusion of a basing relation, the addition of discursive epistemic value changes the character of the theory. For epistemic goodness is no longer all about *you* being in a better relation to the truth. It is also about being in a better relation to other cognizers. Your belief may be better or worse because, say, other people have discovered that their earlier evidence was misleading, and so coming to appreciate your earlier testimony. So the compound theory is not a truth-monist theory. It does not satisfy the requirement that truth be the *only* fundamental explainer of epistemic value. Other cognizers also play that role.

To take a dramatic example, suppose that you are the only one to notice the machinations of a powerful imperfect evil deceiver. In this case, your perceptual evidence may strongly support that everyone else is being deceived.[236] But your evidence for that will not be very influential. For when you attempt to tell people that they are being deceived about this or that, the weight of their evidence means that they should discredit your testimony.[237] So, although your belief is in a better relation to the truth, you are missing out on discursive epistemic value. But then, later, when they come to notice the deceiver's activities, your testimony will become more influential, and so too your beliefs. But *your* relation to the truth hasn't changed! What has changed is the relation of *others* to the truth. And it is those facts about other cognizers that make a difference to the discursive epistemic value of your belief. So, on the compound theory, truth is not the only fundamental

---

[236] For the sake of simplicity, I've restricted the relevant cognizers to *actual* cognizers. But we need not; we might also include many cognizers who *would* be fooled by the imperfect evil deceiver, and get the same result.

[237] Things might be different if you told them they were being deceived about *everything*. Perhaps their evidence would not discredit your testimony in that case. But things are different when we take particulars.

explainer of epistemic value.

References

Ackrill, J. L. 2001. "Aristotle on *Eudaimonia*," in his *Essays on Plato and Aristotle*. Oxford: OUP.
Alloy, Lauren & Abramson, Lyn. 1988 "Depressive realism: Four theoretical perspectives." In Alloy, Lauren, ed., *Cognitive Processes in Depression*. New York: Guilford Press.
Alston, William 2005. *Beyond justification: dimensions of epistemic evaluation*. Ithaca: Cornell UP.
Berker, Selim unpublished. "Epistemic Teleology and the Separateness of Propositions."
Bonjour, Laurence 1985. *The Structure of Empirical Knowledge*. Cambridge, MA: Harvard UP.
Brady, Michel 2009. "Curiosity and the Value of Truth" in Haddock et al. 2009.
Carter, J. Adam & Chrisman, Matthew 2012. "Is epistemic expressivism compatible with inquiry" *Philosophical Studies* 159(3):323-339.
Carter, J. Adam & Jarvis, Benjamin forthcoming. "Against Swamping." *Analysis*. Available at: https://docs.google.com/open?id=0B5Hb33_dHxMBZklselF4UllSYzA
Chisholm, Roderick 1957. *Perceiving: a philosophical study*. Ithaca: Cornell UP.
Chisholm, Roderick 1991. "Firth and the Ethics of Belief." *Philosophy and Phenomenological Research* 51(1):119-128.
Craig, Edward 1999. *Knowledge and the State of Nature, an essay in conceptual synthesis*. Oxford: OUP.
Crimmins, Mark 1992. "I falsely believe that p." *Analysis* 52:191.
David, Marian 2001. "Truth as the Epistemic Goal," in Steup, Matthias, ed. *Knowledge, Truth, and Duty*. Oxford: OUP.
David, Marian 2005. "Truth as the Primary Epistemic Goal: a working hypothesis," in *Contemporary Debates in Epistemology*, Steup, Matthias & Sosa, Ernest, eds. Oxford: Blackwell.
De Almeida, Claudio 2001. "What Moore's Paradox is About," *Philosophy and Phenomenological Research* 62:33-58.
Evnine, Simon 2001. "Learning from one's mistakes: Epistemic Modesty and the Nature of Belief." *Pacific Phil. Quarterly* 82(2):157-177.
Fallis, Don 2007. "Collective Epistemic Goals." *Social Epistemology* 21(3): 267-280.
Fantl, Jeremy & McGrath, Matthew 2002. "Evidence, pragmatics, and justification." *Phil. Review* 111(1):67-94.
Feldman, Richard & Conee, Earl 1985. "Evidentialism." *Phil. Studies* 48: 15-35, reprinted in Feldman & Conee 2004.
Feldman, Richard 2000. "The Ethics of Belief" in *Philosophy and Phenomenological Research* 60: 667-95, reprinted in Feldman and Conee 2004.
Feldman, Richard 2004. "Comments on DeRose's 'Single Scoreboard Semantics'", *Phil. Studies* 119(1/2): 23–33.
Feldman, Richard & Conee, Earl, eds. 2004. *Evidentialism*. Oxford: OUP.
Firth, Roderick 1981. "Epistemic Merit, Intrinsic and Instrumental." *Proceedings and addresses of the APA* 55(1):5-23.
Fitelson, Branden 1999. "The Plurality of Bayesian Measures of Confirmation and the Problem of Measure Sensitivity," *Philosophy of Science* 66(supplement): S362-S378.
Fitelson, Branden 2010. "Strengthening the case for knowledge from falsehood." *Analysis* 70(4): 666-669.
Foley, Richard 1987. *The Theory of Epistemic Rationality*. Cambridge, MA: Harvard UP.
Foley, Richard 1992. *Working without a net: a study of egocentric epistemology*. Oxford: OUP.
Foley, Richard 2001. "The Foundational Role of Epistemology in a General Theory of Rationality"

in *Virtue Epistemology*, Fairweather, Abrol & Zagzebski, Linda, eds. Oxford: OUP.
Fricker, Miranda 2008. "The value of knowledge and the test of time" in *Epistemology: Royal Institute of Philosophy Supplement*, vol. 64, O'Hear, Anthony, ed. Cambridge: CUP.
Fumerton, Richard 1995. *Metaepistemology and Skepticism*. London: Rowman & Littlefield.
Gibbard, Alan 1990. *Wise choices, apt feelings*. Cambridge, MA: Harvard UP.
Gillies, Anthony 2001. "A new solution to Moore's Paradox," *Phil. Studies* 105:237-250.
Goldman, Alvin & Olsson, Erik 2009. "Reliabilism and the value of knowledge" in Haddock et al. 2009.
Greco, John 2009, "The Value Problem," in Haddock et al. 2009.
Green, Mitchell & Williams, John 2007a. *Moore's Paradox: New Essays on Belief, Rationality, and the First Person*. Oxford: Clarendon.
Green, Mitchell & Williams, John 2007b. "Introduction" in Green & Williams 2007a.
Grimm, Stephen 2009. "Epistemic Normativity" in Haddock et al. 2009
Haddock, Adrian & Millar, Alan & Pritchard, Duncan 2009. *Epistemic Value*. Oxford: OUP.
Hájek, Alan 2007. "My philosophical position says ⟨p⟩ and I don't believe ⟨p⟩." In Green & Williams 2007a.
Hawthorne 2004. *Knowledge and Lotteries*. Oxford: OUP.
Hawthorne, John & Bovens, Luc 1999. "The preface, the lottery, and the logic of rational belief." *Mind* 108(430):241-264.
Hitchcock, Christopher 1995. "The mishap at Reichenbach fall: singular vs. general causation," *Phil. Studies* 78:257-291.
Hintikka, Jaako 1962. *Knowledge and Belief: An Introduction to the Logic of the Two Notions*. Ithaca: Cornell UP.
Huber, Franz 2008. "Assessing Theories, Bayes Style." *Synthese* 161(1):89-118.
Jones, Ward 1997. "Why do we value knowledge?" *American Phil. Quarterly* 34(4):423-439.
Kelly, Thomas 2003. "Epistemic Rationality as Instrumental Rationality: A Critique." *Philosophy and Phenomenological Research* 66(3): 612-640.
Kelly, Thomas 2006. "Evidence." Stanford Encyclopedia of Philosophy: http://plato.stanford.edu/entries/evidence/
Kolodny, Niko 2005. "Why be rational?" *Mind* 114(455):509-563.
Kriegel, Uriah 2004. "Moore's Paradox and the Structure of Conscious Belief," *Erkenntnis* 61:99-121.
Kripke, Saul 1979. "A Puzzle about Belief." In *Meaning and Use*, Margalit, A. ed. Dordrecht: Reidel.
Kvanvig, Jonathan 2003. *The Value of Knowledge and the Pursuit of Understanding*. Cambridge: CUP.
Kvanvig, Jonathan 2005. "Truth is not the Primary Epistemic Goal." In Steup & Sosa 2005.
Kvanvig, Jonathan 2008. "Pointless Truth." *Midwest Studies in Philosophy* 32(1):199-212.
Laudan, Lawrence 1981. A confutation of convergent realism. Philosophy of Science 48: 19–49.
Lycan, William 1985. "Epistemic Value." *Synthese* 64(2): 137-164.
Mackie, J.L. 1977. *Ethics: inventing right and wrong*. New York: Penguin.
Malcolm, Norman 1995. "Disentangling Moore's Paradox," in his *Wittgensteinian Themes*. Ithaca: Cornell UP.
McKay, Ryan & Dennett, Daniel 2009. "The Evolution of Misbelief." *Brain and Behavioral Sciences* 32(6):493-510.
Moore, G.E. 1944. "Moore's Paradox." In *G.E. Moore: Selected Writings*. Baldwin, Thomas, ed. London: Routledge.
Olsson, Erik 2011. "Reply to Kvanvig on the Swamping Problem." *Social Epistemology* 25(2):173-182.

Pagin, Peter 2008. "Informativeness and Moore's Paradox." *Analysis* 68(297): 46-57.
Plato 1903. *Platonis Opera*, John Burnet, ed. Oxford: Clarendon.
Priest, Graham 1998. "What is so bad about contradictions?" *The Journal of Philosophy* 95(8):410-426.
Pritchard, Duncan 2010. "Knowledge and Understanding" in Pritchard, Duncan & Millar, Alan & Haddock, Adrian. *The Nature and Value of Knowledge*. Oxford: OUP.
Pritchard, Duncan 2011. "What is the Swamping Problem" in Reisner & Steglich-Petersen 2011.
Pritchard, Duncan 2012. "The Value of Knowledge," in the Stanford Encyclopedia of Philosophy. http://plato.stanford.edu/entries/knowledge-value/
Reisner, Andrew & Steglich-Petersen, Asbjørn, eds. 2011. *Reasons for Belief*. Cambridge: CUP.
Ryan, Sharon 1991. "The Preface Paradox." *Phil. Studies* 64:293-307.
Scott, Dominic 2006. *Plato's* Meno. Cambridge: CUP.
Shoemaker, Sydney 1995. "Moore's paradox and self-knowledge," *Phil. Studies* 77:211-228.
Sorenson, Roy 1988. *Blindspots*. Oxford: OUP.
Stanley, Jason 2005. *Knowledge and practical interests*. Oxford: OUP.
Steglich-Petersen, Asbjørn 2011. "How to be a teleologist about epistemic reasons," in Reisner & Steglich-Petersen 2011.
Steup, Matthias & Sosa, Ernest, eds. 2005. *Contemporary Debates in Epistemology*. Blackwell, Oxford.
Sosa, Ernest 2003. "The Place of Truth in Epistemology." in DePaul, Michael and Zagzebski, Linda, eds., *Intellectual Virtue: Perspectives from Ethics and Epistemology*. Oxford: OUP.
Sosa, Ernest 2010. "Value matters in epistemology." *Journal of Philosophy* 107(4): 167-190.
Van Fraassen, Bas 1980. *The scientific image*. Oxford: OUP.
White, Roger 2005. "Epistemic Permissiveness" *Philosophical Perspectives* 19(1): 445-459.
Williams, Bernard 1973. "Deciding to Believe" in *Problems of the Self*. Cambridge: CUP.
Williams, J. N. 2004. "Moore's Paradoxes, Evans's Principle and Self-Knowledge."*Analysis* 64:348-53.
Williamson, Timothy 2000. *Knowledge and Its Limits*. Oxford: OUP.
Wittgenstein, Ludwig 1958. *Philosophical Investigations*. Oxford: Blackwell.
Wittgenstein, Ludwig 1980. *Remarks on the Philosophy of Psychology* vol. 1. Oxford: Blackwell.
Zagzebski, Linda 1996. *Virtues of the Mind*. Cambridge: CUP.
Zagzebski, Linda 2004. "Epistemic Value Monism," in *Ernest Sosa: And His Critics*, ed. Greco, John. Oxford: Blackwell.

Appendix

Any philosophically respectable theory must be such that someone can rationally adopt a belief in it. But if a theory denies that there are epistemic values, it cannot be rationally adopted. Hence no philosophically respectable theory denies that there are epistemic values.

If a theory T0 denies that there are epistemic values, it entails that:[238]

(1) For any epistemic evaluation EE, EE is false.

But on any characterization of epistemic evaluations:

(2) "For any subject S and theory T, it's rational for S to adopt a belief in T" is an epistemic evaluation

So from (1) and (2) it follows that:

(3) "For any subject S and theory T, it's rational for S to adopt a belief in T" is false

and by disquotation, it follows from (3) that:

(4) For any subject S and theory T, it's not rational for S to adopt a belief in T

and by instantiation, it follows from (4) that:

(5) For any subject S, it's not rational for S to adopt a belief in T0.

And it seems to me that any theory which entails (5), is such that (5) is actually true of it. But (5) isn't true for the reasons that might be given for (1); rather, it's true because the theory is self-defeating. Hence any theory which denies that there are epistemic values - i.e. any T0 - cannot be rationally adopted.

It may be that proponents of (1) who did not realize that it entails (5) can believe (1) *blamelessly* - but this seems to me not a defense of the rationality of such a person adopting (1), and it is certainly not a defense of the philosophical respectability of (1). Since, in the end, what I care about is the philosophical respectability of the theory, I'm happy to substitute some other epistemic status as a middle term in this argument, rather than "can be rationally adopted by someone." Perhaps "can be rationally adopted by someone who recognizes consequences which are at least as easy to draw out as (5) is from (1)" would do the job.

This argument doesn't show, of course, that an anti-realist has to adopt anything like a commonsense view of epistemic evaluations. If truth-monism were revisionary, but not objectionably so, then the anti-realist might simply plump for truth-monism and a moderate error theory. But if the argument of Chapter 4 is right, then truth monism is objectionably revisionary, and so does not hold out the promise it appears to have, for the anti-realist or anyone else.

---

238 Theories which deny bivalence are exceptions to (1), of course, but this won't affect the dialectical strength of the argument.

Milton Keynes UK
Ingram Content Group UK Ltd.
UKHW022249011223
433643UK00012B/1192